THE BREAD BOOK

THE BREAD BOOK

ÉRIC KAYSER

PHOTOGRAPHY BY MASSIMO PESSINA
ORIGINAL RECIPE EDITING BY RÉGIS GARNAUD

FOREWORD

Le Larousse du Pain, later released in English as *The Larousse Book of Bread,* was published in French in 2013. The purpose of the book and its recipes was to lead the way for 'real bread', made using traditional leavening techniques so dear to our predecessors. As consumers become more savvy and conscientious, there's a thriving movement for people to reclaim their food, control ingredients that go into them and take responsibility for what they eat. Inspired by the notion that food is medicine, *Le Larousse du Pain* came about as a response to the growing demands.

Master baker Éric Kayser rose to the challenge, sharing the classic recipes that have brought Maison Kayser great success since its inception in 1996 and enabling baking novices to make his breads at home. Translated into eight languages and with nearly 200,000 copies, the book has helped many home cooks to develop new skills, expand their repertoire and further the cause! By using simple and readily available ingredients, a new generation learned to make starters, to knead dough and to become full-fledged bakers.

The Bread Book continues the journey of discovery begun in *The Larousse Book of Bread*. This exciting new collection proudly builds on the principals that made a success of his first book. While the bread-making techniques remain the same, the (re)discovery of ancient and heritage flours has opened up an entirely new field of opportunities and extraordinary flavours to be explored. This book features new loaves of breads with unexpected flavour profiles to suit all tastes and dietary requirements. Here, readers will find more than sixty classic recipes made with a range of flours, from high-protein lentil flour and chickpea flour to low-gluten varieties made with einkorn, spelt or rye. Beautifully photographed by Massimo Pessina, all recipes can be re-created with ease in home kitchens, using a handful of quality ingredients and basic tools.

For Éric Kayser, taste is the quintessence of good baking. Whether it's Kamut® bread, hemp bread or babka, readers can expect to find goodness, flavour and integrity at the heart of every Maison Kayser loaf.

I hope you enjoy the recipes on the following pages and knead your way to the world of bread!

INTRODUCTION

12	FLOUR TYPES
18	BASIC INGREDIENTS
20	LEVAIN (STARTER)
24	ESSENTIAL EQUIPMENT
26	STAGES OF BREAD-MAKING
28	FOLDING
29	PRE-SHAPING
30	SHAPING
34	SCORING
38	THE BAKER'S LEXICON
40	BREAD-MAKING CHECKLIST

CLASSIC BREADS

44	BOULE
48	BAGUETTE
50	TABATIERE
54	WHOLEMEAL BREAD
56	NO-KNEAD BREAD
58	WREATH
62	CASSEROLE BREAD
64	RYE LOAF
66	THREE-GRAIN LOAF
68	EINKORN BREAD
72	SPELT AND SEED BREAD
74	BUCKWHEAT AND SEED BREAD
76	DANISH BREAD
78	NORWEGIAN BREAD
80	SESAME BREAD
82	HERITAGE WHEAT BREAD
86	ZIGZAG BREAD

BREADS WITH HERITAGE GRAINS

90	RICE FLOUR AND BUCKWHEAT BREAD
92	CHESTNUT BREAD
94	CORN AND SUNFLOWER SEED BREAD
96	GRAPE SEED BREAD
98	SEMOLINA BREAD
102	BRAN LOAF
104	LUPIN AND ALMOND BREAD
106	KAMUT® BREAD
108	SPELT BREAD
112	LENTIL AND CHICKPEA FLOUR BREAD
114	HEMP BREAD
116	QUINOA FLOUR BREAD
118	SWEET POTATO FLOUR BREAD

BREADS OF THE WORLD

- 122 PIZZA
- 124 BURGER BUNS
- 126 BAO
- 130 NAAN
- 132 PITTA
- 134 BAGEL
- 138 TORTILLA
- 140 ROSEMARY FOCACCIA
- 144 CIABATTA WITH SUN-DRIED TOMATOES AND BASIL
- 146 CHALLAH
- 148 FOUGASSE WITH GOAT CHEESE
- 150 THE TWIST

STUFFED LOAVES

- 156 CHEESE BREAD
- 158 WALNUT AND BUTTER BREAD
- 162 OLIVE BREAD
- 166 WALNUT, HAZELNUT AND TURMERIC BREAD
- 168 FIG, HAZELNUT AND FENNEL BREAD
- 172 FLOWER BREAD
- 174 MIXED FRUIT AND NUT CROWN
- 176 MATCHA AND CANDIED ORANGE BREAD
- 178 DATE AND CURRY BREAD

BRIOCHES

- 182 PAIN AU LAIT
- 184 WHITE CHOCOLATE BRIOCHE
- 186 CHOCOLATE AND BANANA BRIOCHE
- 190 PLAITED (BRAIDED) BRIOCHE
- 196 EKMEK WITH RAISINS AND PECANS
- 197 CHOCOLATE AND COCONUT EKMEK
- 200 VIENNA BREAD WITH CHOCOLATE CHIPS
- 202 BABKA
- 206 COCONUT BRIOCHE
- 208 JAPANESE MILK BREAD WITH WHITE CHOCOLATE
- 209 JAPANESE MILK BREAD WITH PISTACHIOS AND CHERRIES

- 215 INDEX BY RECIPE
- 217 INDEX

INTRODUCTION

FLOUR TYPES

WHEAT FLOUR

Did you know that there are thousands of wheat varieties? Of these, durum wheat and common wheat, also known as bread wheat, are the varieties we use the most. Once the seeds – known as berries or kernels – are ground, we can use the resulting flour to make bread, pastries, cakes, pastas and so much more. But how do we make sense of all the different types of wheat flours?

Wheat flour is simply the result of milling wheat berries, regardless of the variety.

As the meaning of its name indicates, durum wheat has hard, glass-like berries that are difficult to grind into fine flour. When crushed, the coarse flour is known as semolina (farina). Durum wheat semolina is used to make certain compact breads, typically mixed with other flours, such as the delicious Semolina Bread (see page 98).

> **WHAT ABOUT KAMUT® FLOUR?**
>
> Kamut®, or khorasan wheat, is an ancient variety of durum wheat from Egypt. This high-protein flour has a pronounced flavour and can be used on its own or mixed with wheat flour, such as in Kamut® Bread (see page 106).

On the other hand, common wheat is easy to grind and produces very fine flour, which are very frequently used for bread-making and pastry-making. This type of flour can also create an airy crumb, making it ideal for brioche-style breads.

Many types of flour are made from common wheat. In France, flour types are classified by the amount of the bran removed from the kernels before milling. (The bran is the outer layer of the berry and has a high mineral content.) To determine this, small flour samples are incinerated at a very high temperature (900°C/1650°F) and the ash residue is then measured. The percentage is used to determine the type of flour.

> **WHOLEMEAL (WHOLE WHEAT) FLOURS: USE ORGANIC**
>
> The darker flours (French T80, T110 and T150 flours) retain part or all of their bran, which is likely to have come into contact with pesticides or insecticides. When sourcing wholemeal (whole wheat) flours, look for products from organic or integrated farming.

The lower the type (T) number, the 'whiter' or more refined the flour will be. In other words, its ash, or mineral, content will be lower. The higher the type number, the higher the bran content, with the highest being wholemeal (whole wheat).

Here are six popular wheat flours used in France, along with their closest equivalent for each flour type.

* Cake/pastry flour (T45 or *farine de gruau*) is a very fine flour made from high-quality common wheat. It contains more gluten than all-purpose flour, which makes it more elastic, and it also has a higher protein content, which gives it a greater ability to rise. It is ideal for pastry recipes and to make leavened doughs when mixed with bread flour, as in the Ciabatta (see page 144) and Date and Curry Bread (see page 178).

* Plain (all-purpose) flour (T55) is very white.
* White bread flour (T65) flour, with its high fibre and mineral content, is recommended for everyday bread.
* Light wholemeal (whole wheat) flour (T80) is ideal for making rustic loaves, such as farmhouse and multigrain bread. Because it is more difficult to work with, it is rarely used in pastry-making.
* Wholemeal flour (T110) is used to make dense loaves. It can be used on its own or mixed with other flours.
* Dark wholemeal (whole wheat) flour (T150) contains all of its bran and makes very dense breads. It can be used alone or mixed with a whiter flour (such as Norwegian Bread on page 78) or with a wheat-free flour (such as Lupin and Almond Bread on page 104).

*

The French classification system is generally used for soft wheat, but it also applies to flours made from other grains, such as rye, einkorn wheat and spelt.

Regardless of flour type, try to use organic when available.

*

> **GLUTEN CONTENT**
>
> Even within the same type of flour, the protein and gluten content can vary. Flours are therefore classified according to their gluten content: the higher the gluten content, the stronger the flour. This means that the gluten network formed during the dough development process will be able to hold its shape more.

WHAT ABOUT OTHER FLOURS?

Here is a non-exhaustive list of flours used in bread-making.

BUCKWHEAT FLOUR
Can be used on its own or mixed in varying proportions with a neutral flour.

BARLEY FLOUR
Barley flour can be used in varying proportions of up to 25 per cent mixed with a neutral flour.

CHESTNUT FLOUR
This flour has a smooth and sweet flavour. It is used in varying proportions of up to 20–50 per cent mixed with a neutral flour.

CHICKPEA (GRAM) FLOUR
Chickpea (gram) flour has a delicate and slightly sweet flavour. It is used in varying proportions of up to 30–40 per cent mixed with a neutral flour. It does not rise at all.

EINKORN FLOUR
With a slightly nutty flavour, einkorn flour can be used in varying proportions of up to 30 per cent mixed with a neutral flour.

GRAPE SEED FLOUR
Use grape seed flour in varying proportions of up to 10–15 per cent mixed with a neutral flour.

LENTIL FLOUR
This flour has a light and sweet flavour. It is used in varying proportions of up to 25 per cent mixed with a neutral flour.

LUPIN FLOUR
Lupin flour has a light and nutty flavour and can be used in varying proportions of up to 30 per cent mixed with a neutral flour. It can also be used as a partial replacement for butter or eggs.

MAIZE FLOUR
Maize flour can be used on its own or in varying proportions. It gives a crumbly and brittle texture.

MILLET FLOUR
While millet flour can be used on its own, it is often mixed with a neutral flour (such as rice flour).

OAT FLOUR
Oat flour, with its slightly sweet taste, can be used in varying proportions of up to 50 per cent mixed with a neutral flour.

QUINOA FLOUR
This flour has a slightly bitter taste. It is used in varying proportions of up to 20–30 per cent mixed with a neutral flour.

RICE FLOUR
This flour has a relatively neutral taste. It is used in varying proportions of up to 50–70 per cent mixed with a neutral flour. It is used to make crumbly products.

RYE FLOUR
Rye flour has a very pronounced rustic flavour. It is used in varying proportions of up to 20–50 per cent mixed with a neutral flour.

SPELT FLOUR
Stronger in flavour than einkorn flour, spelt flour is used in varying proportions of up to 50 per cent mixed with a neutral flour. It is also sometimes used on its own.

SWEET POTATO FLOUR
Use sweet potato flour in varying proportions of up to 50 per cent mixed with a neutral flour.

> MIX THEM UP!
> Whether you're baking bread or pastries, try experimenting with different combinations of grains and flours.

GLUTEN OR GLUTEN-FREE?

These flours contain gluten:
* Barley flour
* Kamut® flour
* Rye flour
* Spelt flour
* Wheat flour

These flours are gluten-free:
* Buckwheat flour
* Chestnut flour
* Chickpea (gram) flour
* Lentil flour
* Lupin flour
* Maize flour
* Millet flour
* Oat flour (gluten-free)
* Quinoa flour
* Rice flour (white or brown)
* Sweet potato flour

SEEDS

Add seeds, grains or nuts to your breads for a crunchy texture and original flavours.

* Chia seeds
* Hemp seeds
* Linseed
* Poppy seeds
* Pumpkin seeds
* Sesame seeds
* Sunflower seeds

As well as…
* Almonds
* Hazelnuts
* Pecans
* Popcorn
* Rolled oats
* Walnuts

BASIC INGREDIENTS

Bread is deceptively easy to make. You only need five key ingredients for the basis of most recipes: flour, water, salt, yeast and levain.

FLOUR
All breads need flour and not necessarily wheat. While breads have been commonly made with wheat flours, we are now spoilt for choice with a wide range of options to suit different tastes and dietary requirements. No matter what flour you use, a delicious loaf of bread must always start with quality ingredients. To find out more, see page 12.

WATER
You want to use a pure water free of impurities. And while spring water is ideal, bottled water is damaging to our environment. In my bakery, we use softeners to purify tap water. At home, consider using a water filter jug (pitcher) or attach a filter to the tap.

SALT
I prefer an unrefined salt with a high mineral content and little iodine such as Guérande sea salt or another artisan sea salt equivalent. An unrefined salt generally comes in flakes or crystals and contains all its minerals, such as magnesium.

LEVAIN (STARTER)
Making bread with a natural starter involves maintaining a balance between the actions of bacteria and yeasts. A levain (starter) is used to make bread rise. Available in liquid or stiff form, it is prepared with varied proportions of water and flour. A liquid levain is prepared by mixing 50 g (scant ½ cup) flour with 50 g (scant ¼ cup) water, while 30 g (2 tablespoons) water is sufficient for a stiff levain. Instructions for making your own levain can be found on page 20.

DEHYDRATED LEVAIN
If pressed for time, you can use a dehydrated starter instead. Available in health food shops, this starter is activated on contact with water in the mixing bowl. It can replace liquid levain, but it's worth noting that the baker's yeast it contains can partially impair the development of the levain.

FRESH YEAST
Fresh yeast serves to support and boost the action of the levain, not to replace it. Crumble it into the mixture of flour and water, taking care that it does not come into contact with salt. It can be found at a bakery or in the refrigerated aisle of a supermarket and kept in the refrigerator between 0 and 10°C (32 and 50°F).

OTHER INGREDIENTS
Seeds (page 16), cheese, dried fruit, sugar, flavoured oils (such as olive, sesame, hazelnut), milk or honey can introduce different flavours and textures to your breads. The possibilities are endless! For optimum results, use only quality ingredients.

LEVAIN (STARTER)

LIQUID AND STIFF LEVAINS

I have always used liquid levain (or liquid sourdough starter) for my breads and pastries. This natural leavener, made of flour and water and regularly refreshed, is inherently tied to our history of breadmaking and fundamental to the earliest practices. Sadly, baking with natural leaveners such as liquid levain was largely eschewed by modern bakers in the twentieth century who preferred to use yeast, which was 'easier' to control and enabled them to produce leavened breads in a very short amount of time. However, these breads have less flavour and a shorter shelf life than those made with levain.

If you want to replace a liquid levain with a dehydrated sourdough starter, you will need about 75 g (2¾ oz) dehydrated starter for every 150 g (⅔ cup/5 oz) liquid levain.

LIQUID LEVAIN
Makes about 700 g (3 cups/1 lb 9 oz)

DAY 1 (IMAGE 1)
In a bowl, whisk 50 g (3½ tbsp/1 ¾ oz) warm water with 50 g (⅓ cup/1¾ oz) organic stoneground wholemeal (whole wheat) flour (T150).

Cover with a cloth and leave to ferment for 24 hours at room temperature (20–25°C/68–77°F).

DAY 2 (IMAGE 2)
In a bowl, whisk together 100 g (scant ½ cup/3½ oz) warm water with 100 g (⅔ cup/3½ oz) organic white bread flour (T65) and 20 g (1 tbsp/¾ oz) honey. Mix this into the previous day's mixture. Cover with a cloth and leave to ferment for 24 hours at room temperature.

DAY 3 (IMAGE 3)
In a bowl, whisk 200 g (1¼ cups/7 oz) organic white bread flour (T65) with 200 g (scant 1 cup/7 oz) warm water. Mix this into day 2's preparation. Cover with a cloth and leave to ferment for 12 hours at room temperature. The liquid levain is ready to be used.

Generally, the levain will remain active for 2 days after it's been refreshed or fed. You will have to feed it every 2 days by adding 50 per cent of its weight in water and flour. For example, if you have 300 g (1¼ cups/10½ oz) levain, add 75 g (½ cup/2¾ oz) flour and 75 g (⅓ cup/2¾ oz) water.

Levain can be stored in an airtight container in the refrigerator for up to 8 days. It must be fed a day before use.

> YEAST
> At the right amount, fresh yeast can complement the levain in most of the recipes in this book. It enhances the fermentation process and sometimes offsets the marked sourness of certain levains.

1

2

3

STIFF LEVAIN
Makes about 650 g (1 lb 7 oz)

DAY 1 (IMAGE 1)
In a bowl, whisk 60 g (¼ cup/2¼ oz) water at 30°C (86°F) and 60 g (½ cup/2¼ oz) organic rye flour. Cover with a cloth and leave to ferment for 24 hours at room temperature (20–25°C/68–77°F).

DAY 2 (IMAGE 2)
In a bowl, whisk together 50 g (3½ tbsp/1¾ oz) water at 30°C (86°F) and 100 g (⅔ cup/3½ oz) light wholemeal (whole wheat) flour (T80), preferably organic, and 20 g (1 tbsp/¾ oz) honey. Mix this into Day 1's mixture. Cover with a cloth and leave to ferment for 24 hours at room temperature.

DAY 3 (IMAGE 3)
In a bowl, mix 250 g (2 cups/9 oz) organic light wholemeal (whole wheat) flour (T80) and 135 g (generous ½ cup/4¾ oz) water at 30°C (86°F) by hand. Mix this into Day 2's preparation. Cover with a cloth and leave to ferment for 12 hours at room temperature. The stiff levain is ready to be used.

The levain can be stored in an airtight container in the refrigerator for up to 8 days. It must be fed a day before use.

ESSENTIAL EQUIPMENT

Certain items of equipment are required to make the bread recipes in this book. You may already have many of these at home.

BAKER'S LAME OR GRIGNETTE
A baker's lame, or grignette, is a tool with a razor-sharp blade at one end, used to score bread dough (and helps control the expansion of the loaf as it bakes). You can use a well-sharpened knife instead, but you run the risk of tearing the dough.

BAKING (PARCHMENT) PAPER
Baking (parchment) paper is used to line baking sheets.

BANNETONS
Available from specialist retailers and on the Internet, these wicker, cloth-lined proving (proofing) baskets come in handy when making certain breads. You can also make do by lining a bowl with a clean cloth dusted with flour.

CLOTHS AND DISH TOWELS
Baker's cloths are heavy linen cloths, used for proving (proofing) dough or rolls. They are slightly dampened before being placed over the bowl or directly over rolls. Alternatively, you could use a clean, heavyweight dish towel.

DIGITAL SCALES
I've provided cup measurements throughout, but my preference when making bread is to weigh all ingredients accurately with a digital scale (i.e. flours may be packed differently).

DOUGH SCRAPER
When kneading by hand, a dough scraper is useful for scraping the dough from the work counter. It can also be used to scrape dough out of a bowl and off your fingers.

MIXING BOWLS
Large mixing bowls are used to mix ingredients.

PANS AND MOULDS
In some instances, shaped pans or moulds can help to create a specific shape or optimise proving (proofing). The specific equipment required is provided in the recipes.

SMALL UTENSILS
Rubber spatulas, spoons, a rolling pin (to roll out dough), a pastry brush (to brush the bread with oil or a glaze), a sieve and scissors are all useful.

STAND MIXER
While nothing compares to the therapeutic benefits of hand-kneading dough, stand mixers make the process infinitely easier and quicker. When using a stand mixer, make sure that the dough hook reaches the bottom of the bowl – otherwise, the dough may not be uniformly mixed.

STAGES OF BREAD-MAKING

1. MIXING AND KNEADING
In this first step in making bread, ingredients are mixed in a stand mixer (or in a bowl for hand kneading). Kneading is done at different speeds.

2. FIRST RISE
During the first rise, also known as bulk fermentation, the dough is covered with a cloth to prevent a crust from forming. Fermentation at room temperature causes the dough to increase in volume as the carbon dioxide produced in the process attempts to escape. In general terms, the dough should double in volume.

The duration of this stage depends on the flour(s) used and the temperature of the room. The dough can be folded halfway through or at the end of this stage to give it greater elasticity (see page 28).

3. DIVIDING AND SHAPING
Once the dough has risen, it is time to divide the dough into pieces if you're making multiple loaves. A dough scraper and digital scales come in handy at this stage to ensure the pieces are of equal weight.

After dividing, the dough pieces are quickly folded to make shaping easy and then loosely shaped, a step known as pre-shaping. See more on page 29.

4. BENCH REST (OPTIONAL)
This optional resting stage makes the dough more supple after it's been divided, which makes it easier to shape. This stage usually has a short duration.

5. FINAL SHAPING
This step is where you give the bread its final shape and a smooth appearance. Different shaping techniques are used, depending on the desired shape. See more on page 30.

6. PROVING (PROOFING)
After the final shaping, dough is covered with a cloth and left to rest at room temperature. The dough again rises and the carbon dioxide creates an open crumb structure. This is also the time to preheat the oven. The end of preheating should coincide with the end of proving (proofing).

7. SCORING (OPTIONAL)
The dough can be scored before baking. Using a baker's lame, make a shallow cut into the surface to allow steam to escape. There are different ways of scoring. See more on page 34.

8. BAKING
Once the oven is preheated, it is time to bake the bread. To keep the bread from drying out as it bakes, it is important to add water to a hot baking pan on the lower rack of the oven.

Baking time will vary, depending on the size and type of bread, and your bread should be regularly checked.

9. REMOVING AND COOLING
Once the bread is baked, carefully remove it from the oven and cool on a wire rack to allow the steam and carbon dioxide to escape.

1

3

6

8

INTRODUCTION

FOLDING

Fold the dough either halfway through or at the end of the first rise, or at both times. It introduces air to the dough to give it body and tightens the gluten network to make the dough firmer, more elastic and smoother. This makes shaping easier and the bread retains its shape as it bakes.

1. On a floured work counter, gently stretch the dough with your hands and then fold one side into the middle.

2. Fold the other sides in the same way, as if making an envelope.

3. Continue to fold the sides into the middle to form a ball.

4. The edges of each fold should no longer be visible.

PRE-SHAPING

After the dough rises, it is divided into individual pieces and given a rough shape, in a stage known as pre-shaping. When pre-shaping, the dough should be worked as little as possible and left to rest before final shaping.

PRE-SHAPING INTO A BOULE

On an unfloured work counter, quickly roll the dough piece over. With the seam underneath, shape into a round ball. When working with small dough pieces, simply roll them under your palms.

PRE-SHAPING INTO AN ELONGATED LOAF

On an unfloured work counter, flatten the dough and roll it back and forth.

PRE-SHAPING INTO A RECTANGLE

On an unfloured work counter, flatten the dough and fold the sides over each other. Turn the dough piece over so that the seam is underneath and press the dough downwards to create a well-proportioned rectangular, or pavé, loaf.

SHAPING

BOULE

1. Carefully flatten the dough piece.
2. Fold the first side into the middle and press gently.
3. Fold the other side in the same way.
4. Roll the dough over with your palms so that the seam is underneath, then rotate it while pulling downwards to tighten and form a boule.

SHAPING

BÂTARD

1. Carefully flatten the dough piece.
2. Fold over a third of the dough and press with your fingers. Turn the dough piece 180 degrees, then fold over another third, like a letter, and press.
3. Fold it in half lengthways and seal the edges with the heel of your hand.
4. Roll it with your palms into an oval shape with tapered ends or a more elongated shape, depending on preference.

SHAPING

BAGUETTE

1. Carefully flatten the dough piece.
2. Fold over a third of the dough and press with your fingers. Turn the dough piece 180 degrees, then fold over another third, like a letter, and press.
3. Fold it in half lengthways and seal the seam with the heel of your hand.
4. Roll it with your palms into an elongated shape and taper the ends.

SHAPING

PAVÉ

1. Carefully flatten the dough piece.
2. Fold over a third of the dough and press with your fingers. Turn the dough piece 180 degrees, then fold over another third, like a letter, and press.
3. Fold it in half lengthways and seal the seam with the heel of your hand.
4. Roll the ends lightly with your hands to seal.

SCORING

THE CROSS CUT

THE SAUSAGE CUT

1. Cut a straight slash across the middle of the loaf.
2. Cut a perpendicular slash across the first to form a cross.

1. Cut a slash diagonally from one end of the loaf to the other.
2. Cut a series of evenly spaced, parallel slashes along the length of the loaf.

SCORING

THE SQUARE CUT

1. Cut two parallel slashes on the sides of the loaf.

2. Cut parallel slashes on the other sides of the loaf perpendicular to the first to make a square.

SCORING

THE LEAF CUT

1. Cut a series of evenly spaced, diagonal slashes over one half of the loaf.

2. Score the other side of the loaf symmetrically to create a leaf pattern.

SCORING

THE DIAMOND (CROSS-HATCH) CUT

1. Cut a series of evenly spaced, diagonal slashes along its length.

2. Start again at the end of the loaf and score in the other direction.

THE BAKER'S LEXICON

ASH CONTENT
A measure used in France to determine a flour's type, it indicates the mineral residue of a flour after incineration at 900°C (1650°F) (see page 12).

AUTOLYSE
A technique consisting of kneading only water and flour, then letting this mixture rest for up to several hours at room temperature. This process adds flexibility and elasticity to the dough.

BANNETON
A wicker basket with a cloth lining used for proving (proofing) dough pieces.

BÂTARD
A shape of a loaf that is neither round nor long, also known as an oblong loaf (see page 31).

BODY
Said of a dough that lacks flexibility.

BOULE SHAPING
Giving a dough piece the shape of a ball, known as a boule, after dividing.

CONSISTENCY
Can be stiff/firm or soft/supple. The consistency of the dough is very important because it affects the development of the bread.

COOLING
Period during which the bread cools and continues to release moisture after removing from the oven.

COVER
Place a cloth or cling film (plastic wrap) over a dough to prevent it from forming a skin.

CUT
See Slash on page 39.

DEFLATING
Also known as knocking back or degassing, this refers to the removal of some of the carbon dioxide from a dough piece by flattening it when shaping, causing it to lose volume.

DIVIDING
Cutting dough into pieces of equal weight and shape.

ELONGATING
Give the dough its final length after tightening.

FERMENTATION
The biochemical transformation of sugars in an oxygen-deprived (anaerobic) environment. Under the action of yeasts and with the aid of enzymes, the micro-organisms convert carbon dioxide and alcohol (ethanol) and the carbon dioxide gas is what makes the dough inflate and therefore 'rise'. The fermentation process is divided into two stages: first rise (bulk fermentation) and proving (proofing). See more on page 26.

FINAL SHAPING
Giving dough its final shape.

FIRST RISE
Also known as bulk fermentation, this is the first stage of the dough's fermentation process. It begins at the end of kneading and ends with shaping.

FLOURING
Lightly dusting dough or a work counter to stop dough from sticking.

FOLDING
Folding the dough to tighten the gluten network and improve elasticity. The dough acquires more strength and develops more uniformly during the proving (proofing) and baking process.

GLAZING
Applying a liquid, such as beaten egg or milk, to create an attractive or glossy finish to a crust.

GREASING
Applying a thin coating of butter or oil to the sides of a loaf pan or baking pan to prevent bread from sticking.

HUMIDIFY
Pouring a small amount of water (50 ml/3½ tbsp/1¾ fl oz) into a hot baking pan and adding it, along with the dough, to the oven in order to produce steam during the baking process.

KNEADING
Working a dough by hand or in a stand mixer with a dough hook in order to develop its strength (flexibility, elasticity and tenacity).

LEVAIN
Also known as leaven, this is a mixture of flour and water, with or without the addition of salt, that undergoes a natural acidifying fermentation.

MOISTENING
Technique that consists of adding water during the mixing process.

OVEN SPRING
The swelling of the dough within the first few minutes of baking.

PAVÉ
Pavé is a small, rustic bread with a cobble-stone shape.

POOLISH
A liquid pre-ferment made from a mixture of equal parts water and flour, to which fresh yeast is added.

PROVING (PROOFING)
The second fermentation period after the dough is shaped and continues until it is baked.

REFRESH
Maintain or feed a levain by adding water and flour.

RESTING
Also known as bench rest. Once the dough is divided and before final shaping, the dough continues to ferment and become more supple.

ROLLING OUT
Flattening dough with a rolling pin to a given thickness.

SCORING
Making one or more slashes into the dough to allow the carbon dioxide to escape when baking (see page 26).

SCRAPE
Roughly clean the sides of a container with a bowl scraper.

SEAM
The line formed where the edges of the dough meet.

SHEET
Dough stretched thinly with a rolling pin or by hand.

SIFT
To remove lumps from a flour by shaking it horizontally in a sieve.

SKINNING
The process by which dough that has been left in contact with the air without the protection of a cloth or a cling film (plastic wrap) forms a skin.

SLASH
A cut made into a dough piece before putting it into the oven. Also known as a cut (see page 38).

STRENGTH
The strength of a dough is characterized by its elasticity and extensibility. If it lacks strength, it will be too stretchy, and if it has too much strength, it will be too elastic and difficult to work with.

INTRODUCTION

BREAD-MAKING CHECKLIST

YOUR KITCHEN TEMPERATURE
The temperature of the ingredients and of your kitchen will impact the fermentation process. In winter, the ideal temperature of the kitchen should be between 20 and 25°C (68 and 77°F), as should all raw ingredients such as flour, water (in a bottle or jug/pitcher) and eggs. In the summer, however, the kitchen should have the coolest possible ambient temperature. If it is very hot, the water and eggs should be kept in the refrigerator. This will lower the temperature of the dough at the end of the mixing and kneading process and slow down the fermentation process.

A PREHEATED OVEN
Bread and pastries should always be put into a hot oven. It is therefore essential to preheat the oven. Make sure to keep to the temperatures indicated in the recipes because baking too slowly at a low temperature will affect the oven spring and flavour of the loaf, and produce a very tight and heavy crumb.

ACCURATE MEASUREMENTS
While I have provided cup measurements in the book, my preference is to weigh everything. Invest in a scale and measure everything in either metric or imperial to prevent conversion errors. I also advise you to weigh out all the ingredients before you start any bread recipe.

FRESH YEAST
Fresh yeast is a living organism. You should therefore always keep it in the refrigerator – up to ten days in its original packaging or a for a few days in an airtight container once opened. To be effective, it should be creamy, crumble perfectly between your fingers and have a pleasant smell.

SALT
Salt is essential as it regulates fermentation, helps bread and pastries rise and enhances flavour and colour when baked.

FLOUR CHOICE
While it may be tempting to use the flour you have in your cupboard, always use the flour specified in the recipe. If not, you run the risk of having a dough that is too soft and impossible to shape. For example, I recommend a high-gluten flour for making bread or pastries.

WATER AMOUNT
This is a very common mistake when making dough. The amount of water will vary depending on the quality of your flour. The older your flour or the lower its quality, the more water it will absorb. To avoid using too much water when mixing and kneading, never pour all of your water into the bowl or mixer when mixing and kneading. Set aside 15–20 per cent and gradually add the remaining water, while checking the consistency of your dough.

TROUBLESHOOT

When bread-making doesn't go accordingly, learn to identify the issue and prevent it from happening again.

Is the dough too sticky?
* Too much water was added during the mixing and kneading stage, or it was too warm.
* The dough has not been mixed and kneaded correctly.

Is the crumb too compact?
* The first rise (bulk fermentation) stage was too short.
* The dough was excessively shaped.
* The dough was incorrectly scored.
* The oven temperature was too high, or more steam was needed.

Does the bread lack volume?
* The flour was too strong.
* The dough was too cold.
* The dough was excessively shaped.
* The dough formed a skin.
* The dough needed to be proved (proofed) longer.
* The dough was incorrectly scored.
* The oven temperature was too high or too low, or more steam was needed.

Did the scoring pattern not hold?
* The scoring was too shallow or the scoring tool was unsuitable.
* The dough was mixed and kneaded incorrectly.
* The dough was excessively or insufficiently shaped.
* There was too much oven spring.
* The oven temperature was too high, or more steam was needed.

Is the crust on the bread soft?
* The dough was too cold.
* The dough was insufficiently shaped.
* The bread was undercooked.
* There was too much steam when the dough went into the oven.
* The bread was not properly cooled after it was removed from the oven.

Is the underside of the bread burnt?
* The oven temperature was too high.
* The baking sheet was positioned too low.

CLASSIC BREADS

BOULE

MAKES 1 boule

PREPARATION TIME 10 min

RESTING TIME 3 h 30 min–4h

BAKING TIME 40–45 min

INGREDIENTS

* 500 g (scant 4 cups/1 lb 2 oz) all-purpose (plain) flour (T55)
* 350 g (1½ cups/12 oz) water at 20°C (68°F)
* 100 g (scant ½ cup/3½ oz) Liquid Levain (see page 20)
* 2 g (½ tsp) fresh yeast, crumbled
* 10 g (2 tsp) Guérande sea salt

1. Put the flour on a work counter or in a mixing bowl and make a large well in the middle. Pour in half the water, then add the levain, yeast and salt. Mix well, then add the remaining water and blend until all the flour is incorporated. Knead the dough until it becomes smooth and elastic (a). Alternatively, put all the ingredients into a stand mixer fitted with a dough hook. Mix and knead for 4 minutes on low speed, then for 6 minutes on high speed, until smooth and elastic.

2. Gather the dough into a ball, cover with a damp cloth and rest for 1½ to 2 hours at room temperature. The dough will have increased in volume by the end of the resting time (b).

3. Place the dough on a lightly floured work counter. Turn it over, then bring the edges in towards the middle (c) and press them down gently. Turn the dough over again and shape it between your hands, while pressing down on the work counter, to create a well-rounded ball (d). Cover with a damp cloth and prove (proof) for 2 hours at room temperature.

4. Place a baking pan on the lowest oven rack and preheat the oven to 230°C (450°F). Transfer the dough to a baking sheet lined with baking (parchment) paper. Score the surface in a cross-hatch pattern. Once the oven is hot, pour 50 ml (3½ tbsp/1¾ fl oz) water into the hot baking pan. Place the loaf and pan of water into the oven and bake for 40–45 minutes.

5. Remove the loaf from the oven, then cool on a wire rack.

a

b

c

d

BAGUETTE

MAKES 3 baguettes

PREPARATION TIME 15 min

RESTING TIME 4 h 40 min

BAKING TIME 20 min

EQUIPMENT

* Baker's cloth

INGREDIENTS

* 500 g (scant 4 cups/1 lb 2 oz) all-purpose (plain) flour (T55)
* 325 g (1⅓ cups/11½ oz) water at 20°C (68°F)
* 100 g (scant ½ cup/3½ oz) Liquid Levain (see page 20)
* 3 g (1 tsp) fresh yeast, crumbled
* 10 g (2 tsp) Guérande sea salt

1 Put the flour and water into a stand mixer fitted with a dough hook and mix for 4 minutes on low speed. Cover the mixer bowl with a damp cloth and rest for 1 hour, then add the levain, yeast and salt. Knead for 4 minutes on low speed, then for 7 minutes on high speed. The dough should be smooth and pull away from the sides of the bowl. Gather the dough into a ball, cover with a damp cloth and leave to rest for 1½ hours at room temperature. The dough will have increased in volume by the end of the resting time.

2 On a floured work counter, divide the dough into three equal pieces. Fold each piece over on itself, pulling gently to stretch into a longish log. Cover with a damp cloth and rest for 30 minutes at room temperature.

3 Working with one piece of dough at a time, use the palm of your hand to flatten it gently. With the long side facing you, fold in a third towards the middle and press along the edge with your fingertips. Swivel the dough 180 degrees. Fold in the other long edge so that it overlaps in the centre and press with the heel of your hand. Fold one half on top of the other and seal the edges together with the heel of your hand.

4 With lightly floured hands, roll the baguette out to 55 cm (21 inches) long, then pinch each end into a point. Repeat with the other 2 baguettes.

5 Carefully lift the baguettes onto a lightly floured baker's cloth, seams underneath. Separate them by making folds in the cloth. Cover with a damp cloth and prove (proof) for 1 hour 40 minutes at room temperature, by which time the baguettes will have increased in volume.

6 Place a baking pan on the lowest rack of the oven and preheat the oven to 230°C (450°F). Gently place the baguettes, seam down, on a baking sheet lined with baking (parchment) paper. Dust with flour and make 4 evenly spaced oblique slashes along the length of each baguette. Once the oven is hot, pour 50 ml (3½ tbsp/1¾ fl oz) water into the hot baking pan. Put the baguettes and pan of water into the oven and bake for 20 minutes.

7 Remove the loaves from the oven, then cool on a wire rack.

TABATIERE

MAKES 3 loaves

PREPARATION TIME 16 min

RESTING TIME 3 h 45 min

BAKING TIME 20 min

INGREDIENTS

* 500 g (scant 4 cups/1 lb 2 oz) plain (all-purpose) flour (T55)
* 325 g (1⅓ cups/11½ oz) water at 20°C (68°F)
* 100 g (scant ½ cup/3½ oz) Liquid Levain (see page 20)
* 4 g (1⅓ tsp) fresh yeast, crumbled
* 10 g (2 tsp) Guérande sea salt
* rye flour (T130), for dusting

1 In a stand mixer fitted with a dough hook, combine the flour and water. Mix for 5 minutes on low speed. Cover the mixer bowl with a damp cloth and rest for 1 hour at room temperature. Add the levain, yeast and salt and knead for 4 minutes on low speed, then for 7 minutes on high speed, until the dough is smooth and pulls away from the sides of the bowl. Gather the dough into a ball and cover with a damp cloth. Leave to rest for 45 minutes at room temperature. The dough will have increased in volume by the end of the resting time.

2 On a floured work counter, divide the dough into three equal pieces. Shape into balls, but don't work the dough too much. Cover with a damp cloth and rest for 30 minutes.

3 Turn the balls so the seams are on top. Bring the edges to the middle and press them down gently. Turn the dough over again and roll on the work counter, pressing gently, to form smooth, even-shaped balls. Dust with rye flour.

4 Use a rolling pin to flatten and roll a third of the dough out and away from you, creating a flap around 15 cm (6 inches) long. Dust lightly with rye flour, then bring the flap back over the top of the dough. Place the loaves on a well-floured cloth, flaps underneath. Cover with a damp cloth and prove (proof) for 1½ hours at room temperature.

5 Place a baking pan on the lowest oven rack and preheat the oven to 230°C (450°F). Turn the dough onto a baking sheet lined with baking (parchment) paper, or onto an oiled baking sheet. The flap should now be on top. Score them with a leaf cut (see page 36). Once the oven is hot, pour 50 ml (3½ tbsp/1¾ fl oz) water into the hot baking pan. Put the loaves and pan of water into the oven and bake for 20 minutes.

6 Remove the loaves from the oven, then cool on a wire rack.

WHOLEMEAL (WHOLE WHEAT) BREAD

MAKES 2 loaves

PREPARATION TIME 20 min

RESTING TIME 4 h 45 min – 4 h 50 min

BAKING TIME 40 min

INGREDIENTS

* 350 g (2¾ cups/12 oz) dark wholemeal (whole wheat) flour (T150)
* 150 g (generous 1 cup/5 oz) white bread flour (T65)
* 75 g (⅓ cup/2¾ oz) Liquid Levain (see page 20)
* 9 g (1¾ tsp) Guérande sea salt
* 2 g (½ tsp) fresh yeast, crumbled
* 350 g (1½ cups/12 oz) water at 16°C (60°F) + 50 g (3½ tbsp/1¾ oz) water for moistening

1. Combine all the ingredients, except the water for moistening, in a stand mixer fitted with a dough hook. Mix for 4 minutes on low speed. When a smooth dough forms, raise the speed to high and knead for 8 minutes. When the dough comes away from the sides of the bowl, gradually moisten with the water while kneading for 2–3 minutes on low speed. Transfer the dough to a bowl and cover with a cloth. Leave to rise for about 2½ hours at room temperature, folding after 1 hour.

2. Deflate the dough on a lightly floured work counter. Divide it into two pieces of equal weight (about 480 g/ 17 oz each). Loosely shape into balls. Cover with a cloth and rest for 15–20 minutes at room temperature.

3. Lightly deflate the dough pieces and transfer to a baking sheet lined with baking (parchment) paper. Cover with a cloth and prove (proof) for about 2 hours at room temperature.

4. Place a baking pan on the lowest oven rack and preheat the oven to 250°C (480°F). Turn the loaves over on the baking sheet so that the seam serves in place of scoring when baking. Once the oven is hot, pour 50 ml (3½ tbsp/ 1¾ fl oz) water into the hot baking pan. Put the loaves and pan of water into the oven and bake for 20 minutes. Lower the temperature to 200°C (400°F) and bake for another 20 minutes.

5. Remove the loaves from the oven, then cool on a wire rack.

WHOLEMEAL BREAD

NO-KNEAD BREAD

MAKES 3 loaves

PREPARATION TIME 20 min

RESTING TIME 31 h 15 min

BAKING TIME 40 min

INGREDIENTS

* 500 g (scant 4 cups/1 lb 2 oz) white bread flour (T65)
* 325 g (1⅓ cups/11½ oz) water at 20°C (68°F)
* 9 g (1¾ tsp) Guérande sea salt
* 2 g (½ tsp) fresh yeast, crumbled
* 150 g (5 oz) Stiff Levain (see page 23)

1. The previous day (24 hours before), combine the flour with the water in a stand mixer fitted with a dough hook and mix on slow speed until a smooth dough forms. Cover the mixer bowl with a cloth and rest the dough for 24 hours at room temperature.

2. On the day, add the salt, yeast and levain to the bowl. Mix on low speed until smooth. Transfer the dough to a bowl and cover with a cloth. Leave to rise for about 5 hours at room temperature, folding every hour.

3. On a floured work counter, divide the dough into three pieces of equal weight (about 330 g/11½ oz each). Pre-shape into boules (see page 30). Cover with a cloth and rest for 15 minutes at room temperature.

4. Shape the dough pieces into baguettes (see page 32). Transfer to a baking sheet lined with baking (parchment) paper. Cover with a cloth and prove (proof) for 2 hours at room temperature.

5. Place a baking pan on the lowest oven rack and preheat the oven to 250°C (480°F). Score the baguettes with a single slash along their length. Once the oven is hot, pour 50 ml (3½ tbsp/1¾ fl oz) water into the hot baking pan. Put the baguettes and pan of water into the oven and bake for 20 minutes. Lower the temperature to 220°C (425°F) and bake for another 20 minutes.

6. Remove the loaves from the oven, then cool on a wire rack.

WREATH

MAKES 1 wreath

PREPARATION TIME 25 min

RESTING TIME 2 h 45 min

BAKING TIME 25 min

EQUIPMENT

* Couronne (ring) banneton

INGREDIENTS

* 50 g (scant ½ cup/1¾ oz) rye flour (T130) + extra for finishing

* 450 g (3½ cups/1 lb) white bread flour (T65)

* 320 g (1⅓ cups/11¼ oz) water at 20°C (68°F)

* 100 g (scant ½ cup/3½ oz) Liquid Levain (see page 20)

* 4 g (1⅓ tsp) fresh yeast, crumbled

* 9 g (1¾ tsp) Guérande sea salt

1. In a stand mixer fitted with a dough hook, combine all the ingredients. Mix for 4 minutes on low speed and then for 7 minutes on high speed. Gather the dough into a ball. Cover with a cloth and leave to rise for 1 hour at room temperature, folding after 30 minutes.

2. On a floured work counter, divide the dough into six pieces of equal weight (about 155 g/5 oz each) and roll into boules (see page 29). Cover with a cloth and rest for 15 minutes at room temperature.

3. Take the dough pieces and rotate with your palms while pressing downwards (a). Dust them with rye flour, then position a rolling pin on the first ball (a little less than a third of the way from the edge). Press down and roll out to form a tongue-shaped flap about 8 cm (3½ inches) in length (b). Dust with rye flour and then fold the flap over the remainder of the piece (c). Repeat with the other five pieces.

4. Dust a couronne (ring) banneton with bread flour. Arrange the balls inside with the flaps facing outward (d). Make sure they touch each other so that they fuse together as they prove (proof) and form the wreath. Cover the banneton with a slightly damp cloth and prove for 1½ hours at room temperature.

5. Place a baking pan on the lowest oven rack and preheat the oven to 230°C (450°F). Carefully turn the wreath over onto a second baking sheet lined with baking (parchment) paper and sift a little flour on top. Once the oven is hot, pour 50 ml (3½ tbsp/1¾ fl oz) water into the hot baking pan. Put the wreath and pan of water into the oven and bake for 10 minutes. Lower the temperature to 210°C (410°F) and bake for another 15 minutes.

6. Remove the wreath from the oven, then cool on a wire rack.

a

b

c

d

CASSEROLE BREAD

MAKES 1 loaf

PREPARATION TIME 20 min

RESTING TIME 3 h 15 min

BAKING TIME 1 h

EQUIPMENT

* Casserole (Dutch oven)

INGREDIENTS

* 500 g (scant 4 cups/1 lb 2 oz) white bread flour (T65) + extra for finishing

* 325 g (1⅓ cups/11½ oz) water at 16°C (60°F)

* 9 g (1¾ tsp) Guérande sea salt

* 2 g (½ tsp) fresh yeast, crumbled

* 200 g (scant 1 cup/7 oz) Liquid Levain (see page 20)

1. In a stand mixer fitted with a dough hook, mix the flour with the water for a few minutes. Cover the mixer bowl with a slightly damp cloth and rest the dough for 1 hour at room temperature.

2. Add the salt to one side of the mixer bowl and the yeast and levain to the other. Knead for 10 minutes on low speed and then for 3 minutes on high speed. The dough should be smooth and pull away from the sides of the bowl.

3. With slightly wet hands, transfer the dough to a floured work counter and fold once. Cover with a cloth and rest for 1 hour at room temperature.

4. Wet your hands and fold again. Cover with a cloth and rest for 1¼ hours at room temperature.

5. Preheat the oven to 245°C (475°F). Dust the inside of casserole (Dutch oven) with flour or line it with baking (parchment) paper. Fold the dough again, then put it into the casserole. Dust the top of the loaf with flour if desired, then score the surface, slashing cleanly. Cover with a lid and bake for 1 hour.

6. Remove the casserole from the oven, taking care not to burn yourself when lifting the lid. Cool the loaf on a wire rack.

* TIP *
Use a casserole made of cast iron or earthenware (including a tagine). Alternatively, bake the bread in a Pyrex baking dish.

RYE LOAF

MAKES 1 loaf

PREPARATION TIME 20 min

RESTING TIME 5 h 15 min

BAKING TIME 1 h 15 min

EQUIPMENT

* Banneton (optional)

FOR THE LEVAIN

* 30 g (2 tbsp/1 oz) Liquid Levain (see page 20)
* 110 g (1 cup/3¾ oz) rye flour (T130)
* 110 g (scant ½ cup/3¾ oz) water at 40°C (104°F)

FOR THE RYE LOAF

* 500 g (4½ cups/1 lb 2 oz) rye flour (T130) + extra for finishing
* 450–500 g (about 2 cups/1–1 lb 2 oz) water at 55–60°C (130–140°F)
* 15 g (2 tsp/½ oz) honey
* 10 g (2 tsp) Guérande sea salt
* 2 g (½ tsp) fresh yeast, crumbled

1. Prepare the levain. In a stand mixer fitted with a dough hook, mix the levain with the rye flour and water. Cover the mixer bowl with a cloth and rest for 3 hours at room temperature.

2. Add all the ingredients for the rye loaf to the mixer bowl and knead for 8 minutes on low speed. The dough should be 28°C (82°F) by the end of the kneading process. Cover the mixer bowl with a cloth and leave the dough to rise for 2 hours at room temperature.

3. Line a banneton or mixing bowl with a cloth and dust with flour. Lightly shape the dough into a boule (see page 30) and place it in the banneton with the seam underneath. Cover with a cloth and rest for 15 minutes at room temperature.

4. Place a baking pan on the lowest oven rack and preheat the oven to 260°C (500°F). Place the dough on a baking sheet lined with baking (parchment) paper and sift a little flour on top. Once the oven is hot, pour 50 ml (3½ tbsp/1¾ fl oz) water into the hot baking pan. Put the loaf and pan of water into the oven and bake for 40 minutes. Lower the temperature to 220°C (425°F) and bake for another 35 minutes.

5. Remove the loaf from the oven, then cool on a wire rack.

* TIP *
To add fruit, dried fruit or nuts to your loaf – the amount should be no more than 20 per cent of the weight of the dough. See more on page 174.

THREE-GRAIN LOAF

MAKES 2 loaves

PREPARATION TIME 20 min

RESTING TIME 2 h 30 min

BAKING TIME 1 h

EQUIPMENT

* Bannetons (optional)

INGREDIENTS

* 600 g (5¼ cups/1 lb 5 oz) rye flour (T130) + extra for finishing
* 200 g (1⅔ cups/7 oz) buckwheat flour
* 200 g (1⅔ cups/7 oz) einkorn flour (T150)
* 750 g (3 cups/1 lb 10 oz) Liquid Levain (see page 20)
* 650 g (2¾ cups/1 lb 7 oz) water at 55–60°C (130–140°F)
* 18 g (heaping 1 tbsp) Guérande sea salt
* 50 g (generous ⅓ cup/1¾ oz) white bread flour (T65), for finishing

1. In a stand mixer fitted with a dough hook, mix all the ingredients together and knead for 8 minutes on low speed until a soft dough forms. The dough should be about 33°C (91°F) by the end of the kneading process. Cover the mixer bowl with a cloth and leave the dough to rise for 2 hours at room temperature.

2. Line 2 bannetons or bowls with a cloth and dust with flour. On a floured work counter, divide the dough into two pieces of equal weight (about 1.2 kg/ 2 lb 12 oz each). Shape into boules (see page 30) and then place them in the bannetons or bowls with the seam facing upwards. Cover with a cloth and prove (proof) for 30 minutes at room temperature.

3. Place a baking pan on the lowest oven rack and preheat the oven to 250°C (480°F). Place the loaves on a baking sheet lined with baking (parchment) paper and sift a little flour on top. Once the oven is hot, pour 50 ml (3½ tbsp/1¾ fl oz) water into the hot baking pan. Put the loaves and pan of water into the oven and bake for about 45 minutes. Lower the temperature to 200°C (400°F) and bake for another 15 minutes.

4. Remove the loaves from the oven, then cool on a wire rack.

EINKORN BREAD

MAKES 4 loaves

PREPARATION TIME 28 min

RESTING TIME 18 h

BAKING TIME 45–50 min

EQUIPMENT

* 4 small loaf pans, 16 x 10 cm (6¼ x 4 inches)

FOR THE LEVAIN

* 45 g (1½ oz) Liquid Levain (see page 20)
* 135 g (generous 1 cup/4¾ oz) einkorn flour (T150)
* 70 g (scant ⅓ cup/2½ oz) water at 40°C (104°F)

FOR THE EINKORN BREAD

* 500 g (4¼ cups/1 lb 2 oz) einkorn flour (T150)
* 320 g (1⅓ cups/11¼ oz) water at 70°C (158°F)
* 10 g (1½ tsp/¼ oz) honey
* 10 g (2 tsp) Guérande sea salt
* 2 g (½ tsp) fresh yeast, crumbled

1. The previous day, prepare the levain. In a stand mixer fitted with a dough hook, mix the levain, einkorn flour and water. Cover the mixer bowl with a cloth and rest the dough for 3 hours at room temperature.

2. Add the bread ingredients to the mixer bowl and knead for 15 minutes on low speed. The dough should be about 25°C (77°F) by the end of the kneading process. Take the dough out of the mixer, cover with a cloth and rest for 30 minutes.

3. On a floured work counter, fold the dough once. Transfer the dough to a bowl and cover with a cloth. Refrigerate overnight.

4. On the day, divide the dough into four pieces of equal weight (about 330 g/11½ oz each) on a floured work counter. Loosely shape into balls and put them into the greased loaf pans, filling to two-thirds. Cover with a cloth and prove (proof) for 2½ hours at room temperature.

5. Place a baking pan on the lowest oven rack and preheat the oven to 235°C (455°F). Once the oven is hot, pour 50 ml (3½ tbsp/1¾ fl oz) water into the hot baking pan. Put the loaves and pan of water into the oven and bake for 45–50 minutes.

6. Remove the loaves from the oven, then cool on a wire rack.

EINKORN BREAD

SPELT AND SEED BREAD

MAKES 2 loaves

PREPARATION TIME 25 min

RESTING TIME 13 h 45 min

BAKING TIME 1 h 10–15 min

INGREDIENTS

* 10 g (1 tbsp/¼ oz) sesame seeds
* 5 g (2 tsp/⅛ oz) poppy seeds
* 5 g (2 tsp/⅛ oz) linseed
* 5 g (2 tsp/⅛ oz) pumpkin seeds
* 5 g (2 tsp/⅛ oz) sunflower seeds
* 5 g (1½ tsp) fresh yeast, crumbled
* 50 g (1¾ oz) Stiff Levain (see page 23)
* 300 g (1¼ cups/10½ oz) water at 30°C (86°F)
* 9 g (1¾ tsp) Guérande sea salt
* 500 g (4¼ cups/1 lb 2 oz) organic spelt flour (T80) + extra for finishing

1. The previous day, preheat the oven to 180°C (350°F). Put the seeds onto a baking sheet and roast for 10–15 minutes.

2. In a bowl, dissolve the yeast and levain in 50 g (3½ tbsp/1¾ oz) of the water and rest for 15 minutes at room temperature.

3. Reduce the oven temperature to 40°C (104°F). Put the dissolved yeast and levain into a stand mixer fitted with a dough hook and add the remaining water, salt and spelt flour. Mix and knead on low speed for 8 minutes. Add the toasted seeds and mix for another 2 minutes. Turn off the oven (it should cool to 25–30°C/77–86°F). Cover the mixer bowl with a cloth and leave to rise in the oven for 1 hour. The dough should double in volume.

4. On a lightly floured work counter, deflate the dough and then loosely shape it into a ball. Cover with a cloth and refrigerate overnight.

5. On the day, deflate the dough on a lightly floured work counter. Divide it into two pieces of equal weight (each about 440 g/1 lb). Lightly shape the dough pieces into boules (see page 30) and transfer to a baking sheet lined with baking (parchment) paper. Cover with a cloth and rest for 30 minutes at room temperature.

6. Place a baking pan on the lowest oven rack and preheat the oven to 250°C (480°F). Dust the loaves with flour and score them. Once the oven is hot, pour 50 ml (3½ tbsp/1¾ fl oz) water into the hot baking pan. Put the loaves and pan of water into the oven and bake for 35 minutes. Lower the temperature to 230°C (450°F) and bake for another 25 minutes, until the crust is crisp and golden brown.

7. Remove the loaves from the oven, then cool on a wire rack.

SPELT AND SEED BREAD

BUCKWHEAT AND SEED BREAD

MAKES 2 loaves

PREPARATION TIME 20 min

RESTING TIME 5 h 20 min

BAKING TIME 35 min

INGREDIENTS

* 400 g (3 cups/14 oz) white bread flour (T65)
* 100 g (scant 1 cup/3½ oz) buckwheat flour
* 350 g (1½ cups/12 oz) water at 16°C (60°F)
* 9 g (1¾ tsp) Guérande sea salt
* 2 g (½ tsp) fresh yeast, crumbled
* 100 g (scant ½ cup/3½ oz) Liquid Levain (see page 20)
* 100 g (¾ cup/3½ oz) seeds (such as millet, sesame, brown linseed or golden linseed)

1. In a stand mixer fitted with a dough hook, mix the flours with the water. Knead for 5 minutes on low speed. Cover the mixer bowl with a cloth and rest the dough for at least 30 minutes at room temperature.

2. Add the salt, yeast and levain to the mixer and knead for 5 minutes on low speed, then for 5 minutes on high speed. The dough should pull away from the sides of the bowl and form a ball. Add the seeds and knead for 2 minutes on low speed. At this point, the dough should be about 24°C (75°F). Cover the mixer bowl with a cloth and leave the dough to rise for 2½ hours at room temperature, folding after 1½ hours.

3. On a lightly floured work counter, divide the dough into two pieces of equal weight (about 450 g/1 lb each) and loosely shape into balls. Cover with a cloth and rest for 20 minutes at room temperature.

4. Without deflating, shape the dough pieces into bâtard loaves (see page 31). Transfer to a baking sheet lined with baking (parchment) paper and, if desired, score with a diamond cross-hatch (see page 37). Cover with a cloth and prove (proof) for 2 hours at room temperature.

5. Place a baking pan on the lowest oven rack and preheat the oven to 250°C (480°F). Once the oven is hot, pour 50 ml (3½ tbsp/1¾ fl oz) of water into the hot baking pan. Put the loaves and pan of water into the oven and bake for 25 minutes. Lower the temperature to 230°C (450°F) and bake for another 10 minutes.

6. Remove the loaves from the oven, then cool on a wire rack.

DANISH BREAD

MAKES 2 loaves

PREPARATION TIME 20 min

RESTING TIME 1 h 20 min

BAKING TIME 1 h 30 min

EQUIPMENT

* 2 loaf pans, 25 x 11 cm (10 x 4¼ inches)

INGREDIENTS

* 15 g (1½ tbsp) fresh yeast, crumbled
* 500 g (generous 2 cups/1 lb 2 oz) water at 30°C (86°F)
* 350 g (3 cups/12 oz) rye flour (T130)
* 150 g (5 oz) dark wholemeal (whole wheat) flour (T150)
* 9 g (1¾ tsp) Guérande sea salt
* 15 g (2 tsp/½ oz) honey
* 5 g (2 tsp/ ⅛ oz) sunflower seeds
* 5 g (2 tsp/ ⅛ oz) pumpkin seeds
* 5 g (½ tbsp/ ⅛ oz) sesame seeds
* 50 g (⅓ cup/1¾ oz) chopped walnuts
* 50 g (⅓ cup/1¾ oz) chopped hazelnuts
* rolled oats, for finishing

1. Dissolve the yeast in half a glass of the warm water.
2. In a stand mixer fitted with a dough hook, mix the flours with the salt. Add the dissolved yeast and mix on low speed, gradually adding the remaining water. Add the honey and seeds and knead for at least 5 minutes. Add the chopped nuts and knead for another 5 minutes. The dough will be very soft and cannot be shaped by hand, which is normal.
3. Preheat the oven to 30°C (86°F). Line the loaf pans with baking (parchment) paper and fill to halfway with the dough. Turn off the oven, put the loaves inside and leave to rise for 1 hour.
4. Remove the loaves, place a baking pan on the lowest oven rack and preheat the oven to 175°C (345°F). Sprinkle the loaves with rolled oats. Once the oven is hot, pour 50 ml (3½ tbsp/ 1¾ fl oz) water into the hot baking pan. Put the loaves and pan of water into the oven and bake for 1½ hours. Turn off the oven, then rest the bread for 20 minutes inside the oven.
5. Remove the loaves from the oven, cool slightly and turn them out onto a wire rack.

NORWEGIAN BREAD

MAKES 4 loaves

PREPARATION TIME 25 min

RESTING TIME 1–2 h

BAKING TIME 1 h

EQUIPMENT

* 4 loaf pans, 25 x 11 cm (10 x 4¼ inches)

INGREDIENTS

* 400 g (3 cups/14 oz) white bread flour (T65)
* 300 g (2⅓ cups/10½ oz) dark wholemeal (whole wheat) flour (T150)
* 300 g (2½ cups/10½ oz) einkorn flour
* 100 g (¾ cup/3½ oz) seeds (such as sesame or sunflower) + extra for finishing
* 600 g (2½ cups/1 lb 5 oz) water at 16°C (60°F) + 150 g (⅔ cup/5 oz) water for moistening
* 150 g (⅔ cup/5 oz) Liquid Levain (see page 20)
* 25 g (generous 1 tbsp/1 oz) honey
* 20 g (4 tsp) Guérande sea salt
* 10 g (1 tbsp) fresh yeast, crumbled

1. Combine all the ingredients, except the water for moistening, in a stand mixer fitted with a paddle attachment. Mix for 10 minutes, then moisten with the water and knead for 10 minutes. Using a dough scraper or rubber spatula, immediately divide the dough into the loaf pans, filling to just above halfway. Cover with a cloth and leave to rise for 1–2 hours at room temperature, until the dough reaches the top of the loaf pans.

2. Place a baking pan on the lowest oven rack and preheat the oven to 240°C (465°F). Once the oven is hot, pour 50 ml (3½ tbsp/1¾ fl oz) water into the hot baking pan. Sprinkle the loaves with seeds. Put the loaves and pan of water into the oven and bake for 35 minutes. Turn the loaves out of their pans, lower the temperature to 210°C (410°F) and bake for another 25 minutes.

3. Remove the loaves from the oven, then cool on a wire rack.

* TIP *
For a more indulgent loaf, add dried fruits at the end of the kneading process, about 100 g (3½ oz) per 1 kg (2 lb 4oz) of dough.

SESAME BREAD

MAKES 3 loaves

PREPARATION TIME 20 min

RESTING TIME 16–17 h

BAKING TIME 30 min

INGREDIENTS

* 100 g (¾ cup/3½ oz) sesame seeds + extra for finishing
* 350 g (1½ cups/12 oz) water at 16°C (60°F) + 25 g (1 tbsp + 2 tsp/1 oz) water for moistening
* 500 g (scant 4 cups/1 lb 2 oz) white bread flour (T65)
* 100 g (scant ½ cup/3½ oz) Liquid Levain (see page 20)
* 9 g (1¾ tsp) Guérande sea salt
* 3 g (1 tsp) fresh yeast, crumbled
* 40 g (4 tbsp/1½ oz) sesame oil + extra for finishing

1. The previous day, preheat the oven to 240°C (465°F). Put the sesame seeds onto a baking sheet and roast for 10 minutes. Then soak them in 70 g (5 tbsp/2½ oz) water for 12 hours.

2. On the day, combine the flour, remaining water, levain, salt and yeast in a stand mixer fitted with a dough hook. Mix and knead for 5 minutes on low speed and then for 10 minutes on high speed. The dough should be smooth and come away from the sides of the bowl. Gradually add the sesame oil and moistening water, then add the seeds and knead for 2 minutes on low speed. Cover the mixer bowl with a cloth and leave the dough to rise for 3 hours, folding after 1½ hours.

3. On a floured work counter, divide the dough into three pieces of equal weight (about 375 g/13 oz each). Lightly deflate the dough pieces and shape into bâtard loaves (see page 31). Place the dough pieces on a baking sheet lined with baking (parchment) paper, cover with a cloth and prove (proof) for 1½ to 2 hours at room temperature.

4. Place a baking pan on the lowest oven rack and preheat the oven to 250°C (480°F). Once the oven is hot, pour 50 ml (3½ tbsp/1¾ fl oz) water into the hot baking pan. Sprinkle the loaves with sesame seeds. Put the loaves and pan of water into the oven and bake for 20 minutes.

5. Remove the loaves from the oven, brush them with sesame oil and cool on a wire rack.

HERITAGE WHEAT BREAD

MAKES 1 loaf

PREPARATION TIME 20 min

RESTING TIME 15 h 15 min

BAKING TIME 1 h 15 min

INGREDIENTS

* 500 g (3¾ cups/1 lb 2 oz) heritage wheat flour
* 200 g (7 oz) Stiff Levain (see page 23)
* 380 g (1 ⅔ cups/13½ oz) water at 22°C (71°F)
* 10 g (2 tsp) Guérande sea salt

1. The previous day, combine all the ingredients in a stand mixer fitted with a dough hook. Mix and knead for 7 minutes on low speed. Cover the mixer bowl with a cloth and leave the dough to rise for 3 hours at room temperature, folding after every hour.

2. Transfer the dough to a floured work counter and loosely shape into a ball. Cover with a cloth and rest for 15 minutes at room temperature.

3. Shape the dough into a square (a) (b). Line a bowl with a cloth and dust with flour. Put the dough into the bowl with the seam underneath and cover with a cloth. Refrigerate for at least 12 hours (at about 6°C/43°F).

4. On the day, transfer the dough to a baking sheet lined with baking (parchment) paper (c). Place a baking pan on the lowest oven rack and preheat the oven to 250°C (480°F). Score the loaf with a diamond cross-hatch (see page 37) (d). Once the oven is hot, pour 50 ml (3½ tbsp/1¾ fl oz) water into the hot baking pan. Put the loaf and pan of water into the oven and bake for 30 minutes. Lower the temperature to 220°C (425°F) and bake for another 45 minutes.

5. Remove the loaf from the oven, then cool on a wire rack.

a

b

c

d

HERITAGE WHEAT BREAD

ZIGZAG BREAD

MAKES 2 loaves

PREPARATION TIME 10 min

RESTING TIME 3 h 45 min

BAKING TIME 25 min

EQUIPMENT

* Baker's cloth

INGREDIENTS

* 50 g (scant ½ cup 1¾ oz) rye flour (T130)
* 450 g (3½ cups/1 lb) plain (all-purpose) flour (T55)
* 320 g (1⅓ cups/11¼ oz) water at 20°C (68°F)
* 100 g (scant ½ cup/3½ oz) Liquid Levain (see page 20)
* 4 g (1⅓ tsp) fresh yeast, crumbled
* 10 g (2 tsp) Guérande sea salt

1. Put all the ingredients into a stand mixer fitted with a dough hook. Mix and knead for 4 minutes on low speed, then for 6 minutes on high speed, until the dough is smooth and pulls away from the sides of the bowl. Gather the dough into a ball and cover with a damp cloth. Leave to rest for 1½ hours at room temperature. Midway through the rest, deflate the dough by folding it in half. It will have increased in volume by the end of the resting time.

2. On a floured work counter, divide the dough into two equal pieces. Shape into balls, but don't work the dough too much. Cover with a damp cloth and rest for 45 minutes at room temperature.

3. Working with one piece of dough at a time, use the palm of your hand to flatten it gently to a rough oval. With the long side facing you, fold in a third towards the middle and press along the edge with your fingertips. Swivel the dough 180 degrees. Fold in the other long edge so that it overlaps in the centre and press again. Fold one half on top of the other and seal the edges together with the heel of your hand. Flatten with your hands again and dust with flour. Score 8 very deep slashes in a cross-hatch pattern (10 cm/4 inches each direction, see page 37), taking care not to cut right through the dough.

4. Turn the loaves over onto a floured baker's cloth. Cover with another damp cloth and prove (proof) for 1½ hours at room temperature.

5. Place a baking pan on the lowest oven rack and preheat the oven to 230°C (450°F). Invert the loaves onto a baking sheet lined with baking (parchment) paper, scored surface on top. Once the oven is hot, pour 50 ml (3½ tbsp/1¾ fl oz) water into the hot baking pan. Put the loaves and pan of water into the oven and bake for 10 minutes. Lower the temperature to 210°C (410°F) and bake for another 15 minutes.

6. Remove the loaves from the oven, then cool on a wire rack.

BREADS WITH HERITAGE GRAINS

RICE FLOUR AND BUCKWHEAT BREAD

MAKES 2 loaves

PREPARATION TIME 20 min

RESTING TIME 2 h 10 min

BAKING TIME 50 min

EQUIPMENT

* 2 loaf pans, 25 x 11 cm (10 x 4¼ inches)

INGREDIENTS

* 520 g (2 cups plus 3 tbsp/1 lb 3 oz) water at 20°C (68°F)
* 30 g (1½ tbsp/1 oz) honey
* 10 g (1 tbsp) fresh yeast, crumbled
* 300 g (2½ cups/10½ oz) buckwheat flour + extra for finishing
* 12 g (2½ tsp) Guérande sea salt
* 200 g (1⅓ cups/7 oz) rice flour
* 25 g (2½ tbsp/1 oz) hazelnut oil + extra for greasing

1. In a bowl, whisk together the water, honey and yeast. Leave to stand for a few minutes.

2. Whisk in the buckwheat flour, followed by the salt. Incorporate the rice flour into the batter and gently mix with a rubber spatula until smooth. You can also mix the batter in a stand mixer fitted with a paddle attachment. Finally, fold in the hazelnut oil.

3. Divide the batter between the loaf pans greased with hazelnut oil, filling to two-thirds. Cover with a cloth and leave to rise for 2 hours at room temperature. The batter should bubble slightly.

4. Place a baking pan on the lowest oven rack and preheat the oven to 230°C (450°F). Once the oven is hot, pour 50 ml (3½ tbsp/1¾ fl oz) water into the hot baking pan. Sprinkle buckwheat flour over the loaves. Put the loaves and pan of water into the oven and bake for 35 minutes. Turn the loaves out of their pans, lower the temperature to 200°C (400°F) and bake for another 15 minutes (pour more water into the hot baking pan just before returning the loaves to the oven). Check that the loaves are fully cooked by pricking with a knife. There should be slight moisture on the tip of the knife.

5. Remove the loaves from the oven, then cool on a wire rack.

CHESTNUT BREAD

MAKES 3 loaves

PREPARATION TIME 25 min

RESTING TIME 15 h 50 min

BAKING TIME 40 min

INGREDIENTS

* 125 g (1 cup/4½ oz) organic chestnut flour
* 325 g (2½ cups/11½ oz) white bread flour (T65)
* 350 g (1½ cups/12 oz) water at 16°C (60°F)
* 150 g (5 oz) Stiff Levain (see page 23)
* 10 g (2 tsp) Guérande sea salt
* 10 g (1½ tsp/¼ oz) chestnut honey
* 3 g (1 tsp) fresh yeast, crumbled
* 150 g (generous 1 cup/5 oz) chestnuts, roughly chopped

1 The previous day, combine all the ingredients, except the chopped chestnuts, in a stand mixer fitted with a dough hook. Mix and knead for 13 minutes on low speed, then add the chestnut pieces and knead for 2 minutes at the same speed. The dough should be about 24°C (75°F) by the end of the kneading process. Cover the mixer bowl with a cloth and leave the dough to rise for 2 hours at room temperature.

2 On a floured work counter, fold the dough once. Transfer the dough to a bowl and cover with a cloth. Refrigerate overnight.

3 On the day, divide the dough into three pieces of equal weight (about 370 g/13 oz each) on a floured work counter. Roughly shape into balls. Cover with a cloth and rest for 20 minutes at room temperature.

4 Shape the dough pieces into pavé loaves (see page 33). Transfer to a baking sheet lined with baking (parchment) paper. Cover with a cloth and prove (proof) for 1½ hours at room temperature.

5 Place a baking pan on the lowest oven rack and preheat the oven to 240°C (465°F). Once the oven is hot, pour 50 ml (3½ tbsp/1¾ fl oz) water into the hot baking pan. Put the loaves and pan of water into the oven and bake for 40 minutes.

6 Remove the loaves from the oven, then cool on a wire rack.

CORN AND SUNFLOWER SEED BREAD

MAKES 5 loaves

PREPARATION TIME 25 min

RESTING TIME 3 h 50 min

BAKING TIME 25 min

INGREDIENTS

* 300 g (2½ cups/10½ oz) maize flour + extra for finishing
* 700 g (5⅓ cups/1 lb 9 oz) white bread flour (T65)
* 18 g (heaping 1 tbsp) Guérande sea salt
* 5 g (1½ tsp) fresh yeast, crumbled
* 650 g (2¾ cups/1 lb 7 oz) water at 20°C (68°F)
* 100 g (scant ½ cup/3½ oz) Liquid Levain (see page 20)
* 1 egg
* 20 g (1½ tbsp/¾ oz) butter
* 150 g (1 ¼ cups/5 oz) popped popcorn
* 100 g (¾ cup/3½ oz) sunflower seeds

1. In a stand mixer fitted with a dough hook, combine the flours salt, yeast, water, levain, egg and butter. Mix and knead for 5 minutes on low speed, then for 10 minutes on high speed. The dough should be smooth and pull away from the sides of the bowl. Add the popcorn and sunflower seeds and knead for 2 minutes on low speed. Cover the mixer bowl with a cloth and leave the dough to rise for 2 hours at room temperature.

2. On a lightly floured work counter, divide the dough into five pieces of equal weight (about 400 g/14 oz each). Pre-shape the dough pieces to resemble rugby balls. Cover with a cloth and rest for 20 minutes at room temperature.

3. Shape the dough pieces into small baguettes about 30 cm (12 inches) in length (see page 32). Cover with a cloth and prove (proof) for 1½ hours at room temperature.

4. Place a baking pan on the lowest oven rack and preheat the oven to 230°C (450°F). Place the loaves on a baking sheet lined with baking (parchment) paper and lightly dust with a little maize flour. Once the oven is hot, pour 50 ml (3½ tbsp/1¾ fl oz) water into the hot baking pan. Put the loaves and pan of water into the oven and bake for 25 minutes.

5. Remove the loaves from the oven, then cool on a wire rack.

CORN AND SUNFLOWER SEED BREAD

GRAPE SEED BREAD

MAKES 2 loaves

PREPARATION TIME 20 min

RESTING TIME 17 h

BAKING TIME 45 min

EQUIPMENT

* 2 loaf pans, 25 x 11 cm (10 x 4¼ inches)

INGREDIENTS

* 40 g (4 tbsp/1½ oz) golden raisins
* 625 g (generous 2½ cups/1 lb 6 oz) water at 20°C (68°F) + extra for the raisins
* 100 g (generous ¾ cup/3½ oz) grape seed flour
* 800 g (6 cups/1 lb 12 oz) white bread flour (T65)
* 100 g (¾ cup/3½ oz) light wholemeal (whole wheat) flour (T80)
* 300 g (10½ oz) Stiff Levain (see page 23)
* 20 g (heaping 1 tbsp) Guérande sea salt
* 3 g (1 tsp) fresh yeast, crumbled

1. The previous day, soak the raisins in a small bowl of water.
2. On the day, drain the raisins. In a stand mixer fitted with a dough hook, mix the flours with the water. Mix for 5 minutes on low speed. Cover the mixer bowl with a cloth and leave the dough to rise for 1 hour at room temperature.
3. Add the remaining ingredients to the mixer, except the raisins, and knead for 10 minutes on low speed, then for 1 minute on high speed. Add the raisins and mix for 1 minute on low speed. Transfer the dough to a bowl. Cover with a cloth and rest for 2 hours at room temperature, folding after 15 minutes and 45 minutes.
4. Divide the dough into two piececs and put them into the loaf pans, filling them halfway. Cover with a cloth and prove (proof) for 2 hours at room temperature. The dough should reach the top of the pans.
5. Place a baking pan on the lowest oven rack and preheat the oven to 230°C (450°F). Once the oven is hot, pour 50 ml (3½ tbsp/1¾ fl oz) water into the hot baking pan. Put the loaves and pan of water into the oven and bake for 30 minutes. Turn the loaves out of their pans, then lower the temperature to 200°C (400°F) and bake for another 15 minutes.
6. Remove the loaves from the oven, then cool on a wire rack.

SEMOLINA BREAD

MAKES 2 loaves

PREPARATION TIME 20 min

RESTING TIME 4 h 15 min

BAKING TIME 20 min

EQUIPMENT

* Bannetons (optional)

INGREDIENTS

* 375 g (scant 3 cups/13 oz) white bread flour (T65)
* 125 g (¾ cup/4½ oz) semolina (farina)
* 100 g (scant ½ cup/3½ oz) Liquid Levain (see page 20)
* 350 g (1½ cups/12 oz) water at 20°C (68°F)
* 2 g (½ tsp) fresh yeast, crumbled
* 10 g (2 tsp) Guérande sea salt

1 In a stand mixer fitted with a dough hook, combine all the ingredients. Mix and knead for 4 minutes on low speed and then for 7 minutes on high speed. The dough should be supple and smooth. Line a banneton or bowl with a cloth and dust with semolina. Gather the dough into a ball and transfer to the banneton or bowl. Cover with a slightly damp cloth and leave to rise for 2 hours at room temperature. The dough should expand.

2 On a floured work counter, divide the dough into two pieces of equal weight (about 470 g/1 lb each). Loosely shape into balls, cover with a cloth and rest for 15 minutes at room temperature.

3 Shape the dough pieces into pavé loaves (see page 33). Transfer to a baking sheet lined with baking (parchment) paper with the seams facing upwards. Cover with a slightly damp cloth and prove (proof) for 2 hours at room temperature.

4 Place a baking pan on the lowest oven rack and preheat the oven to 230°C (450°F). Once the oven is hot, pour 50 ml (3½ tbsp/1¾ fl oz) water into the hot baking pan. Put the loaves and pan of water into the oven and bake for 20 minutes. The loaves will split open at the seam.

5 Remove the loaves from the oven, then cool on a wire rack.

* TIP *
Be careful not to overbake this bread – the crust should remain light and crisp.

SWEET POTATO FLOUR BREAD (PAGE 118) AND LENTIL AND CHICKPEA FLOUR BREAD (PAGE 112)

BRAN LOAF

MAKES 1 loaf

PREPARATION TIME 10 min

RESTING TIME 2 h 45 min

BAKING TIME 20–25 min

INGREDIENTS

* 150 g (3 cups/5 oz) wheat bran
* 300 g (generous 2 cups/10½ oz) plain (all-purpose) flour (T55)
* 50 g (scant ½ cup/1¾ oz) rye flour (T130)
* 320 g (1⅓ cups/11¼ oz) water at 20°C (68°F)
* 100 g (scant ½ cup/3½ oz) Liquid Levain (see page 20)
* 3 g (1 tsp) fresh yeast, crumbled
* 10 g (2 tsp) Guérande sea salt
* sunflower oil, for brushing

1. Combine all the ingredients in a stand mixer fitted with a dough hook. Mix and knead for 4 minutes on low speed, then for 6 minutes on high speed. Gather the dough into a ball and cover with a damp cloth. Leave to rest for 45 minutes at room temperature. The dough will have increased in volume by the end of the resting time.

2. On a floured work counter, gently reshape the dough into a ball, cover with a damp cloth and rest for 30 minutes at room temperature.

3. Brush the work counter with oil. Turn the ball over so the seam is on top, bring the edges to the middle and press them down gently. Turn the dough over again and roll on the work counter, pressing, to form a smooth ball. The oil will prevent the seam from reopening. Cover the dough with a damp cloth and prove (proof) for 1½ hours at room temperature.

4. Place a baking pan on the lowest oven rack and preheat the oven to 230°C (450°F). Turn out the dough onto a baking sheet lined with baking (parchment) paper, with the seam on top. Once the oven is hot, pour 50 ml (3½ tbsp/1¾ fl oz) water into the hot baking pan. Put the loaf and pan of water into the oven and bake for 20–25 minutes.

5. Remove the loaf from the oven, then cool on a wire rack.

LUPIN AND ALMOND BREAD

MAKES 2 loaves

PREPARATION TIME 15 min

RESTING TIME 2 h

BAKING TIME 40 min

EQUIPMENT

* 2 loaf pans, 25 x 11 cm (10 x 4¼ inches)

INGREDIENTS

* 250 g (1 cup/9 oz) water at 16°C (60°F)
* 10 g (1 tbsp/¼ oz) coconut sugar
* 5 g (1½ tsp) fresh yeast, crumbled
* 200 g (1½ cups/7 oz) dark wholemeal (whole wheat) flour (T150)
* 100 g (generous ¾ cup/3½ oz) lupin flour
* 3 g (½ tsp) Guérande sea salt
* 40 g (¼ cup/1½ oz) almonds + extra for finishing
* 10 g (2 tsp/¼ oz) coconut oil

1. In a stand mixer fitted with a paddle attachment, combine the water, sugar and yeast. Mix for 3 minutes on low speed, then add the flours and salt, and mix and knead for 4 minutes. Add the almonds and coconut oil and mix for another minute. Divide the dough into two pieces and then put them into greased loaf pans, filling to two-thirds. Cover with a cloth and prove (proof) for 2 hours at room temperature.

2. Place a baking pan on the lowest oven rack and preheat the oven to 240°C (465°F). Once the oven is hot, pour 50 ml (3½ tbsp/1¾ fl oz) water into the hot baking pan. Sprinkle almonds on top of the loaves. Put the loaves and pan of water into the oven and bake for 30 minutes. Turn the loaves out of their pans, then lower the temperature to 200°C (400°F) and bake for another 10 minutes.

3. Remove the loaves from the oven, then cool on a wire rack.

KAMUT® BREAD

MAKES 3 loaves

PREPARATION TIME 15 min

RESTING TIME 3 h 30 min

BAKING TIME 25 min

INGREDIENTS

* 300 g (2½ cups/10½ oz) Kamut® flour + extra for finishing
* 200 g (1⅔ cups/7 oz) white bread flour (T65)
* 325 g (1⅓ cups/11½ oz) water at 20°C (68°F)
* 150 g (⅔ cup/5 oz) Liquid Levain (see page 20)
* 10 g (2 tsp) Guérande sea salt
* 1 g (⅓ tsp) fresh yeast, crumbled

1 Combine all the ingredients in a stand mixer fitted with a dough hook. Mix and knead for 4 minutes on low speed and then for 4 minutes on high speed. Gather the dough into a ball, cover with a slightly damp cloth and leave to rise for 1½ hours at room temperature. The dough should expand.

2 On a floured work counter, divide the dough into three pieces of equal weight (about 320 g/11¼ oz each). Roughly shape into balls. Cover with a cloth and rest for 30 minutes at room temperature.

3 Shape the dough pieces into bâtard loaves (see page 31) about 20 cm (8 inches) in length. Transfer to a baking sheet lined with baking (parchment) paper with the seam underneath. Cover with a cloth and prove (proof) for 1½ hours at room temperature.

4 Place a baking pan on the lowest oven rack and preheat the oven to 225°C (435°F). Dust the dough pieces with Kamut® flour through a sieve and cut two slashes. Once the oven is hot, pour 50 ml (3½ tbsp/1¾ fl oz) water into the hot baking pan. Put the loaves and pan of water into the oven and bake for 25 minutes.

5 Remove the loaves from the oven, then cool on a wire rack.

* TIP *
Kamut® flour can be difficult to work, producing a dough with just little rise. To increase your chance of success with this bread, try using a loaf pan.

SPELT BREAD

MAKES 3 loaves

PREPARATION TIME 8 min

RESTING TIME 3 h 30 min

BAKING TIME 30 min

EQUIPMENT

* Baker's cloth

INGREDIENTS

* 325 g (2¾ cups/11½ oz) plain (all-purpose) flour (T55), plus extra for dusting
* 175 g (1½ cups/6 oz) spelt flour
* 310 g (1¼ cups/12 oz) water at 20°C (68°F)
* 150 g (⅔ cup/5 oz) Liquid Levain (see page 20)
* 1 g (⅓ tsp) fresh yeast, crumbled
* 10 g (2 tsp) Guérande sea salt

1. Combine all the ingredients in a stand mixer fitted with a dough hook. Mix and knead for 4 minutes at low speed, then for another 4 minutes at high speed. Gather the dough into a ball. Cover with a damp cloth and leave to rest for 1½ hours at room temperature. The dough will have increased in volume by the end of the resting time.

2. On a floured work counter, divide the dough into three equal pieces. Shape them into balls. Cover with a damp cloth and leave to rest for 30 minutes. Flatten the dough pieces gently.

3. If you wish, you can shape each piece differently (see pages 30–33). To make a boule, place the dough on a lightly floured work surface. Turn it over, then bring the edges in towards the middle and press down lightly (a) (b) (c). Turn the dough over again, then use your hands to shape into a ball (d). Place on a floured baker's cloth, seam upwards. Cover the three shaped loaves with a damp cloth and leave to proof (prove) for 1½ hours. The dough will have increased in volume by the end of the proofing time.

4. Place a baking pan on the lowest oven rack and preheat the oven to 230°C (450°F). Transfer the loaves, seams underneath, onto a baking sheet lined with baking (parchment) paper. Score in a cross-hatch pattern (see page 37). Once the oven is hot, pour 50 ml (3½ tbsp/1¾ fl oz of water into the hot baking pan. Put the loaves and pan of water into the oven and bake for 30 minutes.

5. Remove the loaves from the oven, then cool on a wire rack.

a

b

c

d

LENTIL AND CHICKPEA FLOUR BREAD

MAKES 2 loaves

PREPARATION TIME 20 min

RESTING TIME 4 h 45 min

BAKING TIME 1 h 15 min

INGREDIENTS

* 75 g (⅔ cup/2¾ oz) lentil flour
* 75 g (⅔ cup/2¾ oz) chickpea (gram) flour
* 350 g (2½ cups/12 oz) plain (all-purpose) flour (T55)
* 300 g (1¼ cups/10½ oz) water at 16°C (60°F)
* 20 g (2 tbsp/¾ oz) coconut sugar
* 9 g (1¾ tsp) Guérande sea salt
* 5 g (1½ tsp) fresh yeast, crumbled
* 1 tbsp olive oil

1. Combine all the ingredients in a stand mixer fitted with a dough hook. Mix and knead for 4 minutes on low speed and then for 4 minutes on high speed. Cover the mixer bowl with a cloth and leave the dough to rise for 3 hours at room temperature, folding after 1½ hours.

2. On a lightly floured work counter, divide the dough into two pieces of equal weight (about 420 g/15 oz each). Roughly shape into balls. Cover with a cloth and rest for 15 minutes at room temperature.

3. Shape the dough pieces into boules (see page 30) and transfer to a baking sheet lined with baking (parchment) paper. Cover with a cloth and prove (proof) for 1½ hours at room temperature.

4. Place a baking pan on the lowest oven rack and preheat the oven to 250°C (480°F). Score the loaves with a cross (see page 34). Once the oven is hot, pour 50 ml (3½ tbsp/1¾ fl oz) water into the hot baking pan. Put the loaves and pan of water into the oven and bake for 30 minutes. Lower the temperature to 220°C (425°F) and bake for another 45 minutes.

5. Remove the loaves from the oven, then cool on a wire rack.

LENTIL AND CHICKPEA FLOUR BREAD

HEMP BREAD

MAKES 2 loaves

PREPARATION TIME 15 min

RESTING TIME 14 h 45 min

BAKING TIME 30 min

INGREDIENTS

* 80 g (½ cup/3 oz) hemp seeds
* 325 g (1⅓ cups/11½ oz) water at 16°C (60°F) + 10 g (2 tsp) water for moistening
* 500 g (3¼ cups/1 lb 2 oz) rice flour
* 100 g (scant ½ cup/3½ oz) Liquid Levain (see page 20)
* 9 g (1¾ tsp) Guérande sea salt
* 2 g (½ tsp) fresh yeast, crumbled

1. The previous day, soak the hemp seeds in a bowl with 50 g (3½ tbsp/1¾ oz) of the water.

2. In a stand mixer fitted with a dough hook, combine the remaining water and all the ingredients, except the water for moistening. Mix and knead for 5 minutes on low speed and then for 6 minutes on high speed, gradually moistening with the extra water. The dough must be smooth. Take the dough out of the mixer, gather it into a ball and transfer to a bowl. Cover with a cloth and leave to rise for 1 hour at room temperature, folding after 30 minutes. Then fold again, cover the bowl with cling film (plastic wrap) and refrigerate.

3. On the day, divide the dough into two pieces of equal weight (about 500 g/1 lb 2 oz each) on a floured work counter. Roughly shape into balls. Cover with a cloth and rest for 15 minutes at room temperature.

4. Preheat the oven to 25–30°C (77–86°F). Shape the dough pieces into bâtard loaves (see page 31). Transfer to a baking sheet lined with baking (parchment) paper. Turn off the oven, prove (proof) the loaves inside for 1½ hours and then take them out.

5. Place a baking pan on the lowest oven rack and preheat the oven to 240°C (465°F). Once the oven is hot, pour 50 ml (3½ tbsp/1¾ fl oz) water into the hot baking pan. Score the loaves with a single slash along their length. Put the loaves and pan of water into the oven and bake for 20 minutes. Lower the temperature to 180°C (350°F) and bake for another 10 minutes.

6. Remove the loaves from the oven, turn them out and cool on a wire rack.

QUINOA FLOUR BREAD

MAKES 3 loaves

PREPARATION TIME 20 min

RESTING TIME 3 h 20 min

BAKING TIME 25 min

EQUIPMENT

* 3 loaf pans, 25 x 11 cm (10 x 4¼ inches)

INGREDIENTS

* 125 g (1 cup/4¼ oz) quinoa flour
* 375 g (3 cups/13 oz) organic einkorn flour + extra for finishing
* 320 g (1⅓ cups/11¼ oz) water at 24°C (75°F)
* 100 g (scant 1 cup/3½ oz) Liquid Levain (see page 20)
* 10 g (2 tsp) Guérande sea salt
* 3 g (1 tsp) fresh yeast, crumbled

1. Combine all the ingredients in a stand mixer fitted with a dough hook. Mix and knead for 8 minutes on low speed and then for 3 minutes on high speed. The dough should be about 23–25°C (73–77°F) by the end of the kneading process. Cover the mixer bowl with a cloth and leave the dough to rise for 1½ hours at room temperature, folding after 30 minutes.

2. On a floured work counter, divide the dough into three pieces of equal weight (about 310 g/11 oz each). Roughly shape into balls. Cover with a cloth and rest for 20 minutes at room temperature.

3. Shape the dough pieces into bâtard loaves (see page 31). Place them in greased loaf pans. Cover with a cloth and prove (proof) for 1½ hours at room temperature.

4. Place a baking pan on the lowest oven rack and preheat the oven to 240°C (465°F). Lightly dust the loaves with flour. Once the oven is hot, pour 50 ml (3½ tbsp/1¾ fl oz) water into the hot baking pan. Put the loaves and pan of water into the oven and bake for 25 minutes.

5. Remove the loaves from the oven. Turn them out, then cool on a wire rack.

QUINOA FLOUR BREAD

SWEET POTATO FLOUR BREAD

MAKES 3 loaves

PREPARATION TIME 20 min

RESTING TIME 3 h 30 min–4 h 40 min

BAKING TIME 35 min

INGREDIENTS

* 150 g (generous 1 cup/5 oz) sweet potato flour
* 500 g (scant 4 cups/1 lb 2 oz) white bread flour (T65) + extra for finishing
* 300 g (1¼ cups/10½ oz) water at 16°C (60°F)
* 32 g (2 tbsp/1 oz) Liquid Levain (see page 20)
* 23 g (1¾ tbsp/¾ oz) olive oil + extra for brushing
* 22 g (3 tsp/¾ oz) honey
* 10 g (2 tsp) Guérande sea salt
* 3 g (1 tsp) fresh yeast, crumbled
* 80 g (½ cup/2¾ oz) pumpkin seeds

1. Combine all the ingredients, except the pumpkin seeds and olive oil, in a stand mixer fitted with a dough hook. Mix and knead for 5 minutes on low speed and then on high speed until the dough is smooth and pulls away from the sides of the bowl. Add the pumpkin seeds (set aside a handful for decoration) and knead for 1 minute on low speed. Cover the mixer bowl with a cloth and leave the dough to rise for 1½ hours at room temperature, folding after 1 hour.

2. On a floured work counter, divide the dough into three pieces of equal weight (about 370 g/13 oz each) and loosely shape into balls. Cover with a cloth and rest for 20 minutes at room temperature.

3. Shape the dough pieces into pavé loaves (see page 33). Brush the tops of the loaves with a little water to moisten and sprinkle with the reserved pumpkin seeds. Transfer to a baking sheet lined with baking (parchment) paper. Cover with a cloth and prove (proof) for 1½ to 2 hours at room temperature. The dough should double in volume.

4. Place a baking pan on the lowest oven rack and preheat the oven to 240°C (465°F). Once the oven is hot, pour 50 ml (3½ tbsp/1¾ fl oz) water into the hot baking pan. Put the loaves and pan of water into the oven and bake for about 20 minutes.

5. Remove the loaves from the oven, brush with olive oil and cool on a wire rack.

SWEET POTATO FLOUR BREAD

BREADS
OF
THE WORLD

PIZZA

MAKES 2 large pizzas

PREPARATION TIME 20 min

RESTING TIME 3 h

BAKING TIME 15 min

FOR THE PIZZA

* 500 g (scant 4 cups/1 lb 2 oz) white bread flour (T65)
* 260 g (generous 1 cup/9½ oz) water at 20°C (68°F)
* 100 g (scant ½ cup/3½ oz) Liquid Levain (see page 20)
* 5 g (1½ tsp) fresh yeast, crumbled
* 10 g (2 tsp) Guérande sea salt
* 15 g (1½ tbsp/½ oz) caster (superfine) sugar
* 30 g (2 tbsp/1 oz) olive oil + extra for finishing

FOR THE TOPPING

* 400 g (1¾ cups/14 oz) tomato sauce
* 10 slices ham
* a little dried oregano
* 200 g (scant 2 cups/7 oz) grated Emmental cheese

1. In a stand mixer fitted with a dough hook, combine all the pizza ingredients except the oil. Mix and knead for 5 minutes on low speed and then for 6 minutes on high speed. Incorporate the oil and mix for another 2 minutes. Gather the dough into a ball, cover with a cloth and leave to rise for 2 hours at room temperature, folding after 1 hour. The dough should expand.

2. On a floured work counter, divide the dough into two pieces of equal weight (about 460 g/1 lb each). Use a rolling pin to roll the dough into sheets the same size as a baking sheet. Lay the dough sheets on baking sheets lined with baking (parchment) paper. Prick them all over with a fork, except for a 1-cm (½-inch) wide border around the edges. Cover with a slightly damp cloth and prove (proof) for 1 hour at room temperature.

3. Spread the tomato sauce over the dough, leaving a clear border around the edge. Arrange ham slices on top, then sprinkle with oregano and cheese.

4. Place a baking pan on the lowest oven rack and preheat the oven to 235°C (455°F). Once the oven is hot, pour 50 ml (3½ tbsp/1¾ fl oz) water into the hot baking pan. Put the pizzas and pan of water into the oven and bake for 4 minutes. Lower the temperature to 220°C (425°F) and bake for another 11 minutes.

5. Remove the pizzas from the oven and brush a thin layer of oil over the edges.

* TIP *
To ensure the dough pieces fit the baking sheets, unstick them from the work counter and allow them to shrink to their real size.

BURGER BUNS

MAKES 10 buns

PREPARATION TIME 20 min

RESTING TIME 2 h 45 min

BAKING TIME 14 min

INGREDIENTS

- 500 g (3½ cups/1 lb 2 oz) cake (pastry) flour (T45/farine de gruau)
- 200 g (scant 1 cup/7 oz) water at 16°C (60°F)
- 50 g (3½ tbsp/1¾ oz) Liquid Levain (see page 20)
- 3 egg yolks
- 35 g (3 tbsp/1¼ oz) caster (superfine) sugar
- 25 g (1 oz) milk powder
- 25 g (2 tbsp/1 oz) butter
- 12 g (scant 1½ tbsp/½ oz) fresh yeast, crumbled
- 10 g (2 tsp) Guérande sea salt
- 50 g (3½ tbsp/1¾ oz) sunflower oil + extra for finishing
- sesame seeds, for finishing

* VARIATION 1 *
For tomato-flavoured buns, replace 3½ tbsp water with 3½ tbsp tomato purée (paste).

* VARIATION 2 *
For black burger buns, add squid ink at a proportion of 10 g (¼ oz) per 1 kg (2 lb 4 oz) of dough.

1. Combine all the ingredients, except the oil and sesame seeds, in a stand mixer fitted with a dough hook. Mix and knead for 5 minutes on low speed and then for 10 minutes on high speed. Add the oil on low speed. Cover the mixer bowl with a cloth and rest the dough for 15 minutes at room temperature, then refrigerate for about 30 minutes.

2. On a floured work counter, divide the dough into ten pieces of equal weight (about 100 g/3½ oz each). Shape them into boules (see page 30). Brush them with oil and then dredge the brushed part in the sesame seeds. Transfer to a baking sheet lined with parchment (baking) paper. Cover with a cloth and prove (proof) for 2 hours at room temperature.

3. Place a baking pan on the lowest oven rack and preheat the oven to 170°C (340°F). Once the oven is hot, pour 50 ml (3½ tbsp/1¾ fl oz) water into the hot baking pan. Put the buns and pan of water into the oven and bake for 14 minutes.

4. Remove the buns from the oven, then cool on a wire rack.

BAO

MAKES 12 buns

PREPARATION TIME 25 min

RESTING TIME 2 h 15 min

BAKING TIME 20 min

INGREDIENTS

* 10 g (1 tbsp) fresh yeast, crumbled
* 270 g (1⅓ cups/9½ oz) water at 35°C (95°F)
* 500 g (scant 4 cups/1 lb 2 oz) cake (pastry) flour (T45/farine de gruau)
* 20 g (1½ tbsp/¾ oz) caster (superfine) sugar
* 20 g (1½ tbsp/¾ oz) neutral oil + extra for finishing
* 6 g (1 tsp) Guérande sea salt

1. In a stand mixer fitted with a dough hook, combine the yeast with the water and mix on low speed. Add the flour, sugar, oil and salt, then knead for 10 minutes on very low speed. Gather the dough into a ball. Cover the mixer bowl with a cloth and leave the dough to rise for 1½ hours at room temperature.

2. Preheat the oven to 40°C (104°F). On a floured work counter, divide the dough into 12 pieces of equal weight (about 70 g/2½ oz each) and shape into balls. Use a rolling pin to roll the pieces into ovals (a). Unstick the dough pieces from the work counter and let them shrink naturally. Lay the pieces on a baking sheet lined with baking (parchment) paper. Brush the surface of the dough with a little oil and then lay a rectangular piece of baking paper over a half of each piece (b) (c). Fold the dough in half over the baking paper (d). Turn off the oven and prove (proof) the dough pieces inside for 45 minutes. They should expand well.

3. Take the dough out of the oven, place a baking pan on the lowest rack and preheat the oven to 110°C (225°F). Once the oven is hot, pour 330 ml (scant 1½ cups/11 oz) water into the hot baking pan. Put the buns and pan of water into the oven and bake for 20 minutes. (Alternatively, steam the bao buns. Bring water to the boil in a pan and place a steamer basket lined with baking paper on top. Place the buns in the basket – they should not be touching – cover and cook for about 10 minutes. The steam will cause a thin and shiny film to form.)

a

b

c

d

NAAN

MAKES 9 naans

PREPARATION TIME 20 min

RESTING TIME 3 h

BAKING TIME 5 min each

EQUIPMENT

* Heavy baking sheet or pizza stone

INGREDIENTS

* 120 g (½ cup/4¼ oz) full-fat (whole) milk
* 115 g (scant ½ cup/4 oz) water at 20°C (68°F)
* 10 g (1 tbsp/¼ oz) caster (superfine) sugar
* 5 g (1 tsp) fine salt
* 1 egg
* 470 g (3½ cups/1 lb) white bread flour (T65) + extra for finishing
* 10 g (1 tbsp) fresh yeast, crumbled
* 100 g (scant ½ cup/3½ oz) Liquid Levain (see page 20)
* 45 g (generous 3 tbsp/1½ oz) butter, melted, for finishing

VARIATION 1
To make seeded naans, add a handful of seeds (such as sesame, linseed or poppy seeds) towards the end of the kneading stage.

VARIATION 2
For cheese naans, place a portion of melting cheese on top of the stretched dough piece then fold it over before baking.

1. In a bowl, mix the milk with the water and then add the sugar and salt.

2. In a stand mixer fitted with a dough hook, mix the egg, flour, yeast and levain, then incorporate the water and milk mixture. Knead for 10 minutes on low speed to a smooth dough. Cover the mixer bowl with a cloth and leave the dough to rise for about 2 hours at room temperature. The dough should double in volume.

3. On a floured work counter, divide the dough into nine pieces of equal weight (about 100 g/3½ oz each). Loosely shape into balls and dust the surface with flour. Cover with a cloth and rest for 1 hour at room temperature.

4. Place a heavy baking sheet or pizza stone in the oven, and a baking pan on the lowest rack, and preheat the oven to 240°C (465°F). On a floured work counter, flatten and stretch the dough pieces with your hands, dusting with flour, to form thin crepe-like sheets. Once the oven is hot, pour 50 ml (3½ tbsp/1¾ fl oz) water into the hot baking pan. Place the naans on the hot baking sheet, then put the naans and pan of water into the oven and cook for a few minutes until puffed up and golden on top.

5. Remove the naans from the oven and brush with melted butter.

PITTA

MAKES 7 pittas

PREPARATION TIME 20 min

RESTING TIME 1 h 10 min

BAKING TIME 5–10 min

INGREDIENTS

* 475 g (3⅔ cups/1 lb 1 oz) white bread flour (T65)
* 220 g (scant 1 cup/7¾ oz) water at 16°C (60°F)
* 75 g (⅓ cup/2¾ oz) Liquid Levain (see page 20)
* 45 g (⅓ cup/1½ oz) olive oil
* 25 g (2½ tbsp/1 oz) fresh yeast, crumbled
* 10 g (1 tbsp/¼ oz) caster (superfine) sugar
* 4 g (scant 1 tsp) Guérande sea salt

1. Combine all the ingredients in a bowl and mix them by hand to a smooth paste. Transfer the dough to a floured work counter and knead for about 5 minutes, until smooth. Return the dough to the bowl, cover with a damp cloth and leave to rise for 1 hour at room temperature.

2. Place a baking sheet lined with baking (parchment) paper in the oven and preheat to 240°C (465°F). On a floured work counter, divide the dough into seven pieces of equal weight (about 120 g/4¼ oz each). Roll them out to a thickness of about 1 cm (½ inch). Rest the pittas for 10 minutes at room temperature and then place them on the hot sheet. Bake for 5–10 minutes.

3. The pittas will puff up as they bake and deflate when removed from the oven.

BAGEL

MAKES 9 bagels

PREPARATION TIME 28 min

RESTING TIME 1 h 45 min

BAKING TIME 15 min

INGREDIENTS

* 500 g (scant 4 cups/1 lb 2 oz) white bread flour (T65) + extra for finishing
* 200 g (scant 1 cup/7 oz) water at 20°C (68°F)
* 100 g (scant ½ cup/3½ oz) Liquid Levain (see page 20)
* 5 g (1½ tsp) fresh yeast, crumbled
* 10 g (2 tsp) Guérande sea salt
* 20 g (1½ tbsp/¾ oz) caster (superfine) sugar
* 1 egg + 1 beaten egg for glazing
* 25 g (2 tbsp/1 oz) butter, softened
* poppy and/or sesame seeds, for finishing

1. In a stand mixer fitted with a dough hook, combine all the ingredients except the butter and seeds. Mix and knead for 4 minutes on low speed and then for 4 minutes on high speed. Incorporate the butter and mix for another 3 minutes. Gather the dough into a ball, cover with a slightly damp cloth and leave to rise for 1 hour at room temperature. The dough should expand.

2. Transfer the dough to a floured work counter, deflate and loosely roll into a ball. Divide it into nine pieces of equal weight (about 100 g/3½ oz each). Cover with a cloth and rest for 15 minutes at room temperature.

3. Rotate the dough pieces between your hands to shape into very round boules (a). Dust the tops with flour, then use a finger to make a hole through the middle (b). Gradually stretch the hole to make it wider (c). Cover with a cloth and prove (proof) for 30 minutes at room temperature.

4. Bring water to a simmer in a small pan. Use a skimmer to immerse a dough piece in the simmering water (d). Leave to cook for 1½ minutes and then turn them over and cook for another 1½ minutes. The dough piece will have puffed up. Place on a wire rack over the sink to drain and repeat with the remaining dough pieces.

5. Prepare two large plates, one filled with poppy seeds and the other with sesame seeds. Brush the bagels with beaten egg, then dip half of them in the sesame seeds and half in the poppy seeds (or all in one type of seed if you prefer). Transfer to a baking sheet lined with baking (parchment) paper.

6. Place a baking pan on the lowest oven rack and preheat the oven to 200°C (400°F). Once the oven is hot, pour 50 ml (3½ tbsp/1¾ fl oz) water into the hot baking pan. Put the bagels and pan of water into the oven and bake for 15 minutes.

7. Remove the bagels from the oven, then cool on a wire rack.

a

b

c

d

TORTILLA

MAKES 8 tortillas

PREPARATION TIME 20 min

RESTING TIME 30 min

BAKING TIME 1 min per wrap

INGREDIENTS

* 400 g (scant 3 cups/14 oz) plain (all-purpose) flour (T55)
* 5 g (1 tsp) Guérande sea salt
* 90 g (scant ½ cup/3¼ oz) olive oil
* 150 g (⅔ cup/5 oz) water at 16°C (60°F)

1. In a stand mixer fitted with a dough hook, mix the flour with the salt. Mix and knead on low speed until the dough is smooth and pulls away from the sides of the bowl. Add the oil and knead again. Gradually add the water while kneading at a slow speed until the dough forms a ball that pulls away from the sides of the bowl. Divide the dough into eight small balls of equal weight. Cover with a slightly damp cloth and leave to rest for 30 minutes to 1 hour at room temperature.

2. On a floured work counter, use a rolling pin to roll out the dough balls into very fine crepe-like sheets. Place a dry frying pan or skillet over a high heat and cook the tortillas for 30 seconds on each side (20 seconds per side is usually sufficient after the second tortilla).

3. Let cool. Wrap the tortillas around the filling of your choice and slice off the ends on a diagonal.

ROSEMARY FOCACCIA

MAKES 1 large focaccia

PREPARATION TIME 25 min

RESTING TIME 15 h 30 min

BAKING TIME 15–20 min

INGREDIENTS

* 4–5 sprigs rosemary
* 30 g (3 tbsp/1 oz) olive oil + extra for drizzling
* 500 g (scant 4 cups/1 lb 2 oz) white bread flour (T65)
* 330 g (scant 1½ cups/11½ oz) water at 20°C (68°F)
* 100 g (scant ½ cup/3½ oz) Liquid Levain (see page 20)
* 7 g (2 tsp) fresh yeast, crumbled
* 10 g (2 tsp) fine salt
* pinch of coarse salt

1. The previous day, remove the leaves from the rosemary sprigs and mix them with the olive oil in a bowl. Leave to steep overnight, then strain. Finely chop the rosemary leaves.

2. On the day, combine the flour, water, levain, yeast, fine salt and rosemary leaves in a stand mixer fitted with a dough hook. Mix and knead for 5 minutes on low speed and then for 8 minutes on high speed. Incorporate the rosemary-infused oil and mix for 2 minutes. Gather the dough into a ball. Cover with a damp cloth and leave to rise for 2 hours at room temperature, folding over after 1 hour. The dough should expand.

3. Transfer the dough to a greased baking sheet and spread it out with your fingers until it covers the entire surface (a) (b) (c). Cover with a slightly damp cloth and prove (proof) for 1½ hours at room temperature.

4. Place a baking pan on the lowest oven rack and preheat the oven to 230°C (450°F). Press your fingers into the dough to make dimples all over the surface, then drizzle with a little oil and spread the oil gently over the surface of the dough, using your hands (d). Sprinkle with coarse salt. Once the oven is hot, pour 50 ml (3½ tbsp/ 1¾ fl oz) water into the hot baking pan. Put the focaccia and pan of water into the oven and bake for 15–20 minutes.

5. Remove the focaccia from the oven, then cool on a wire rack.

a

b

c

d

ROSEMARY FOCACCIA

CIABATTA WITH SUN-DRIED TOMATOES AND BASIL

MAKES 3 loaves

PREPARATION TIME 25 min

RESTING TIME 5 h

BAKING TIME 15 min

INGREDIENTS

* 60 g (4¼ cups loosely packed/2¼ oz) fresh basil, chopped

* 250 g (1¾ cups/9 oz) cake (pastry) flour (T45/farine de gruau)

* 250 g (1¾ cups/9 oz) white bread flour (T65)

* 325 g (1⅓ cups/11½ oz) water at 16°C (60°F)

* 100 g (scant ½ cup/3½ oz) Liquid Levain (see page 20)

* 9 g (1¾ tsp) Guérande sea salt

* 3 g (1 tsp) fresh yeast, crumbled

* 30 g (2 tbsp/1 oz) olive oil + extra for finishing

* 100 g (scant 2 cups/3½ oz) sun-dried tomatoes, finely chopped

1 Combine all the ingredients, except the oil and sun-dried tomatoes, in a stand mixer fitted with a dough hook. Mix and knead for 4 minutes on low speed and then for 8 minutes on high speed. Gradually add the olive oil and mix for another 4 minutes. Add the sun-dried tomatoes and mix for 2 minutes on low speed. Cover the mixer bowl with a cloth and leave the dough to rise for 3 hours at room temperature, folding after 1½ hours.

2 On a floured work counter, divide the dough into three pieces of equal weight (about 375 g/13 oz each). Shape the dough pieces into rectangular pavé loaves (see page 33). Transfer to a baking sheet lined with baking (parchment) paper. Cover with a cloth and prove (proof) for 2 hours at room temperature.

3 Place a baking pan on the lowest oven rack and preheat the oven to 250°C (480°F). Once the oven is hot, pour 50 ml (3½ tbsp/1¾ fl oz) water into the hot baking pan. Put the loaves and pan of water into the oven and bake for 15 minutes.

4 Remove the loaves from the oven, brush with olive oil and cool on a wire rack.

CIABATTA WITH SUN-DRIED TOMATOES AND BASIL

CHALLAH

MAKES 3 loaves

PREPARATION TIME 25 min

RESTING TIME 2 h 25 min

BAKING TIME 18 min

INGREDIENTS

* 535 g (generous 4 cups/1 lb 3 oz) white bread flour (T65)
* 290 g (scant 1¼ cups/10¼ oz) water at 16°C (60°F)
* 50 g (¼ cup/1¾ oz) caster (superfine) sugar
* 15 g (1½ tbsp) fresh yeast, crumbled
* 10 g (2 tsp) Guérande sea salt
* 30 g (3 tbsp/1 oz) olive oil
* poppy and sesame seeds, for finishing

1. Combine all the ingredients, except the oil and seeds, in a stand mixer fitted with a dough hook. Mix and knead for 4 minutes on low speed and then for 2 minutes on high speed. Incorporate the oil and mix for another 2 minutes. Cover the mixer bowl with a cloth and rest the dough for 40 minutes at room temperature, then refrigerate for about 30 minutes.

2. On a floured work counter, divide the dough into nine pieces of equal weight (about 100 g/3½ oz each) and pre-shape to resemble rugby balls. Cover with a cloth and rest for 15 minutes at room temperature.

3. Make a plait (braid) using three dough pieces. Repeat the operation with the remaining dough pieces to make three plaits. Sprinkle with poppy seeds and sesame seeds. Transfer to a baking sheet lined with baking (parchment) paper. Cover with a cloth and prove (proof) for 1 hour at room temperature.

4. Place a baking pan on the lowest oven rack and preheat the oven to 160°C (325°F). Once the oven is hot, pour 50 ml (3½ tbsp/1¾ fl oz) water into the hot baking pan. Put the loaves and pan of water into the oven and bake for 18 minutes.

5. Remove the loaves from the oven, then cool on a wire rack.

FOUGASSE WITH GOAT CHEESE

MAKES 4 fougasse

PREPARATION TIME 15 min

RESTING TIME 3 h 15 min

BAKING TIME 18 min

INGREDIENTS

* 500 g (scant 4 cups/1 lb 2 oz) all-purpose (plain) flour (T55)
* 300 g (1¼ cups/10½ oz) water at 20°C (68°F)
* 100 g (scant ½ cup/3½ oz) Liquid Levain (see page 20)
* 5 g (1½ tsp) fresh yeast, crumbled
* 10 g (2 tsp) Guérande sea salt
* 30 g (2 tbsp/1 oz) extra-virgin olive oil + extra for brushing
* 100 g (scant ½ cup/3½ oz) crème fraîche
* 100 g (scant 1 cup/3½ oz) grated Emmental cheese
* 200 g (7 oz) ash goat cheese, sliced

1. Put the flour, water, levain, yeast and salt into a stand mixer fitted with a dough hook. Mix and knead for 5 minutes on low speed, then for 7 minutes on high speed. Add the olive oil and knead for another 3 minutes. Gather the dough into a ball, cover with a damp cloth and leave to rest for 2 hours at room temperature. Midway through the rest, deflate the dough by folding it in half. It will have increased in volume by the end of the resting time.

2. On a floured work counter, divide the dough into four equal pieces. Working with one piece at a time, turn it around on the work counter, bring the edges in to the middle and press down. Turn it again and shape into a ball, tucking the seam underneath. Repeat with the other three pieces of dough, then cover them with a damp cloth and rest for 15 minutes.

3. Use a rolling pin to roll each piece of dough into oval flatbreads, around 40 cm (16 inches) long and about 5 mm (¼ inch) thick. Spread one half of each flatbread with crème fraîche, leaving a 2-cm (¾-inch) border around the edge. Sprinkle with grated Emmental and top with slices of goat cheese.

4. Use a dough cutter to make 3 wide slashes on the ungarnished half of each flatbread, then fold it over the other half. Seal all the edges. Place the fougasse on lightly oiled baking sheets. Cover with a damp cloth and prove (proof) for 1 hour at room temperature.

5. Place a baking pan on the lowest oven rack and preheat the oven to 235°C (455°F). Once the oven is hot, pour 50 ml (3½ tbsp/1¾ fl oz) water into the hot baking pan. Put the fougasse and pan of water into the oven and bake for 4 minutes. Lower the temperature to 220°C (425°F) and bake for another 14 minutes.

6. Remove the fougasse from the oven, brush them lightly with olive oil and cool on a wire rack.

FOUGASSE WITH GOAT CHEESE

THE TWIST

MAKES 3 loaves

PREPARATION TIME 10 min

RESTING TIME 3 h 50 min

BAKING TIME 20 min

INGREDIENTS

* 500 g (scant 4 cups/1 lb 2 oz) plain (all-purpose) flour (T55), plus extra for dusting
* 310 g (scant 1¼ cups/11 oz) water at 20°C (68°F)
* 100 g (scant ½ cup/3½ oz) Liquid Levain (see page 20)
* 4 g (1⅓ tsp) fresh yeast, crumbled
* 10 g (2 tsp) Guérande sea salt

1. Combine all the ingredients in a stand mixer fitted with a dough hook. Mix and knead for 4 minutes on low speed and then for 6 minutes at high speed. Gather the dough into a ball and cover with a damp cloth. Leave to rise for 1½ hours at room temperature. The dough will have increased in volume by the end of the resting time.

2. On a floured work counter, divide the dough into 3 equal pieces (each about 300 g/10½ oz). Fold each piece over on itself, pulling gently to lengthen. Cover with a damp cloth and leave to rest for 30 minutes at room temperature.

3. Working with one ball of dough at a time, use the palm of your hand to flatten it gently. With the long side facing you, fold in a third towards the middle and press with your fingertips. Swivel the dough 180 degrees. Fold in the other edge so that it overlaps in the middle and press again. Fold one half on top of the other and seal the edges together with the heel of your hand.

4. With lightly floured hands, roll the dough out to 40 cm (16 inches). Shape the other loaves in the same way. Leave to rest for 20 minutes. Dust the loaves with flour. Use a rolling pin to press into each loaf along its length (a), then bring the edges together (b). Pick up the ends of the dough and twist gently. Keep one hand still while you twist three times with the other; do this in stages, resting between each twist in order to achieve a neat finish (c) (d).

5. Arrange the loaves on a baking sheet lined with baking (parchment) paper. Cover with a damp cloth and prove (proof) for 1½ hours at room temperature.

6. Place a baking pan on the lowest oven rack and preheat the oven to 230°C (450°F). Invert the loaves so the rolled side is on top. Once the oven is hot, pour 50 ml (3½ tbsp/1¾ fl oz) water into the hot baking pan. Put the loaves and pan of water into the oven and bake for 20 minutes.

7. Remove from the oven, then cool on a wire rack.

a

b

c

d

THE TWIST

STUFFED LOAVES

CHEESE BREAD

MAKES 6 loaves

PREPARATION TIME 20 min

RESTING TIME 4 h 30 min

BAKING TIME 20 min

INGREDIENTS

* 1 kg (7½ cups/2 lb 4 oz) white bread flour (T65)
* 650 g (2¾ cups/1 lb 7 oz) water at 16°C (60°F) + 50 g (3½ tbsp/1¾ oz) water for moistening
* 200 g (scant 1 cup/7 oz) Liquid Levain (see page 20)
* 5 g (1 tsp) fresh yeast, crumbled
* 18 g (heaping 1 tsp) Guérande sea salt
* 370 g (13 oz) Comté cheese, cut into cubes
* 1 egg, beaten, for glazing
* 100 g (scant 1 cup/3½ oz) grated Emmental cheese

1. In a stand mixer fitted with a dough hook, mix the flour with the water (not the water for moistening). Knead for 5 minutes on low speed. Cover the mixer bowl with a cloth and rest the dough for 1 hour at room temperature.

2. Add the levain, yeast and salt. Mix and knead for 4 minutes on low speed and then for 4 minutes on high speed. Gradually add the moistening water and mix for another 3 minutes. Stop the mixer, add the Comté cubes and then knead for 2 minutes on the lowest speed. Cover the mixer bowl with a cloth and leave the dough to rise for 1½ hours at room temperature.

3. On a floured work counter, divide the dough into six pieces of equal weight (about 410 g/14½ oz each). Shape the dough into bâtard loaves (see page 31), without excessive tightening. Transfer to a baking sheet lined with baking (parchment) paper. Glaze the loaves by brushing them with beaten egg and cover the top with the grated Emmental. Cover with a cloth and prove (proof) for 2 hours at room temperature.

4. Place a baking pan on the lowest oven rack and preheat the oven to 230°C (450°F). Once the oven is hot, pour 50 ml (3½ tbsp/1¾ fl oz) water into the hot baking pan. Put the loaves and pan of water into the oven and bake for 20 minutes.

5. Remove the loaves from the oven, then cool on a wire rack.

WALNUT AND BUTTER BREAD

MAKES 5 loaves

PREPARATION TIME 15 min

RESTING TIME 3 h

BAKING TIME 17 min

EQUIPMENT

* Baker's cloth

INGREDIENTS

* 500 g (scant 4 cups/1 lb 2 oz) plain (all-purpose) flour (T55)
* 225 g (scant 1 cup/8 oz) water at 20°C (68°F)
* 100 g (scant ½ cup/3½ oz) Liquid Levain (see page 20)
* 5 g (1½ tsp) fresh yeast, crumbled
* 10 g (2 tsp) Guérande sea salt
* 25 g (¼ cup/1 oz) milk powder
* 35 g (scant ¼ cup/1¼ oz) caster (superfine) sugar
* 75 g (⅓ cup/2¾ oz) softened butter, roughly diced
* 150 g (1½ cups/5 oz) walnuts, chopped

1. Put the flour, water, levain, yeast, salt, milk powder and sugar into a stand mixer fitted with a dough hook. Mix and knead for 5 minutes on low speed, then for 7 minutes on high speed. Mix in the butter and knead for another 3 minutes. Add the walnuts and mix in briefly on low speed. Gather the dough into a ball, cover with a damp cloth and leave to rest for 1½ hours at room temperature. Midway through the rest, deflate the dough by folding it in half. It will have increased in volume by the end of the resting time.

2. On a floured work counter, divide the dough into five equal pieces and shape them into balls. Cover with a damp cloth and rest for 15 minutes.

3. Working with one piece of dough at a time, use the palm of your hand to flatten it gently into a rough oval. With the long side facing you, fold in a third towards the middle and press along the edge with your fingertips. Swivel the dough 180 degrees. Fold in the other long edge so that it overlaps in the middle and press again. Fold one half on top of the other and seal the edges together with the heel of your hand (a). With lightly floured hands, roll the dough out to form a plump oval. Shape the other 4 pieces of dough in the same way.

4. Score the loaves diagonally in a sausage cut (see page 34) (b). Place them, seams underneath, on a floured baker's cloth, separating them by making folds in the cloth (c). Cover with a damp cloth and prove (proof) for 1¼ hours at room temperature.

5. Place a baking pan on the lowest oven rack and preheat the oven to 230°C (450°F). Arrange the loaves seams underneath on a baking sheet lined with baking (parchment) paper. Once the oven is hot, pour 50 ml (3½ tbsp/1¾ fl oz) water into the hot baking pan. Put the loaves and pan of water into the oven and bake for 17 minutes.

6. Remove the loaves from the oven, then cool on a wire rack.

a

b

c

WALNUT AND BUTTER BREAD

WALNUT AND BUTTER BREAD

OLIVE BREAD

MAKES 3 loaves

PREPARATION TIME 25 min

RESTING TIME 4 h 30 min

BAKING TIME 25–30 min

INGREDIENTS

* 500 g (scant 4 cups/1 lb 2 oz) white bread flour (T65)
* 350 g (1½ cups/12 oz) water at 16°C (60°F)
* 100 g (scant ½ cup/3½ oz) Liquid Levain (see page 20)
* 10 g (2 tsp) Guérande sea salt
* 3 g (1 tsp) fresh yeast, crumbled
* 35 g (3½ tbsp/1¼ oz) olive oil
* 150 g (1 cup/5 oz) black and green olives, pitted

1. Combine all the ingredients, except the oil and olives, in a stand mixer fitted with a dough hook. Mix and knead for 5 minutes on low speed and then for 10 minutes on high speed, until the dough is smooth and pulls away from the sides of the bowl. Gradually add the olive oil and incorporate, then add the olives and knead for 2 minutes on low speed. Cover the mixer bowl with a cloth and leave the dough to rise for 2½ hours at room temperature, folding after 1 hour.

2. On a floured work counter, divide the dough into three pieces of equal weight (about 380 g/13½ oz each) and pre-shape to resemble rugby balls.

3. Lightly flatten the dough pieces without deflating (a). Use a knife or dough scraper to make three slashes along the middle (b). Twist the dough pieces (c) (d). Transfer to a baking sheet lined with baking (parchment) paper. Cover with a cloth and prove (proof) for 2 hours at room temperature.

4. Place a baking pan on the lowest oven rack and preheat the oven to 220°C (425°F). Moisten the loaves by brushing with water. Once the oven is hot, pour 50 ml (3½ tbsp/1¾ fl oz) water into the hot baking pan. Put the loaves and pan of water into the pan and bake for 25–30 minutes.

5. Remove the loaves from the oven, then cool on a wire rack.

OLIVE BREAD

a

b

c

d

WALNUT, HAZELNUT AND TURMERIC BREAD

MAKES 4 loaves

PREPARATION TIME 25 min

RESTING TIME 14 h

BAKING TIME 35 min

INGREDIENTS

* 75 g (½ cup/2¾ oz) hazelnuts
* 10 g (1½ tbsp/¼ oz) ground turmeric
* 500 g (scant 4 cups/1 lb 2 oz) white bread flour (T65)
* 275 g (1 cup plus 2 tbsp/9¾ oz) water at 16°C (60°F)
* 75 g (⅓ cup/2¾ oz) butter
* 75 g (⅓ cup/2¾ oz) Liquid Levain (see page 20)
* 35 g (3 tbsp/1¼ oz) caster (superfine) sugar
* 25 g (1 oz) milk powder
* 5 g (1½ tsp) fresh yeast, crumbled
* 9 g (1¾ tsp) Guérande sea salt
* 75 g (⅔ cup/2¾ oz) walnuts

1. The previous day, preheat the oven to 180°C (350°F). Put the hazelnuts onto a baking sheet and roast for 15 minutes. Let cool.

2. On the day, combine all the ingredients, except the nuts, in a stand mixer fitted with a dough hook. Mix and knead for 5 minutes on low speed and then for 10 minutes on high speed. When the dough is smooth and comes away from the sides of the bowl, add the nuts and mix for 2 minutes on low speed. Cover the mixer bowl with a cloth and leave the dough to rise for 45 minutes at room temperature.

3. On a floured work counter, divide the dough into four pieces of equal weight (about 290 g/10¼ oz each) and loosely shape into balls. Cover with a cloth and rest for 15 minutes at room temperature.

4. Shape the dough pieces into small bâtard loaves (see page 31). Transfer the loaves to a baking sheet lined with baking (parchment) paper and score them with a leaf cut (see page 36). Cover with a cloth and prove (proof) for 1½ hours at room temperature.

5. Place a baking pan on the lowest oven rack and preheat the oven to 220°C (425°F). Once the oven is hot, pour 50 ml (3½ tbsp/1¾ fl oz) water into the hot baking pan. Put the loaves and pan of water into the oven and bake for 20 minutes.

6. Remove the loaves from the oven, then cool on a wire rack.

FIG, HAZELNUT AND FENNEL BREAD

MAKES 3 loaves

PREPARATION TIME 20 min

RESTING TIME 17 h 15 min

BAKING TIME 40 min

INGREDIENTS

* 50 g (scant ⅓ cup/1¾ oz) hazelnuts
* 500 g (scant 4 cups/1 lb 2 oz) white bread flour (T65)
* 325 g (1⅓ cups/11½ oz) water at 16°C (60°F) + 25 g (1 tbsp + 2 tsp/1 oz) water for moistening
* 100 g (scant ½ cup/3½ oz) Liquid Levain (see page 20)
* 3 g (1 tsp) fresh yeast, crumbled
* 9 g (1¾ tsp) Guérande sea salt
* 2 g (1 tsp) fennel seeds
* 2 g (2 sprigs) rosemary
* 125 g (4½ oz) dried figs, finely chopped

1. The previous day, preheat the oven to 180°C (350°F). Put the hazelnuts onto a baking sheet and roast for 15 minutes. Let cool.

2. On the day, in a stand mixer fitted with a dough hook, mix the flour with the water (not the water for moistening). Knead for 5 minutes on low speed. Cover the mixer bowl with a cloth and rest the dough for 1 hour at room temperature.

3. Add the levain, yeast, salt, fennel seeds and rosemary. Knead for 4 minutes on low speed and then for 4 minutes on medium speed. Gradually add the moistening water and mix for another 3 minutes. Mix in the hazelnuts and figs for 1 minute on low speed. Cover the mixer bowl with a cloth and leave the dough to rise for 2 hours at room temperature.

4. On a floured work counter, divide the dough into three pieces of equal weight (about 370 g/13 oz each) and loosely shape into balls. Cover with a cloth and rest for 15 minutes at room temperature.

5. Shape the dough pieces into bâtard loaves (see page 31). Transfer to a baking sheet lined with baking (parchment) paper. Cover with a cloth and prove (proof) for 2 hours at room temperature.

6. Place a baking pan on the lowest oven rack and preheat the oven to 250°C (480°F). Score the bread with a sausage cut (see page 34). Once the oven is hot, pour 50 ml (3½ tbsp/1¾ fl oz) water into the hot baking pan. Put the loaves and pan of water into the oven and bake for 15 minutes. Lower the temperature to 220°C (425°F) and bake for another 10 minutes.

7. Remove the loaves from the oven, then cool on a wire rack.

FIG, HAZELNUT AND FENNEL BREAD

CHEESE BREAD (PAGE 156) AND OLIVE BREAD (PAGE 162)

FLOWER BREAD

MAKES 2 loaves

PREPARATION TIME 20 min

RESTING TIME 16 h 15 min

BAKING TIME 30 min

INGREDIENTS

* 200 g (7 oz) edible flowers
* 100 g (scant ½ cup/3½ oz) Liquid Levain (see page 20)
* 400 g (3 cups/14 oz) white bread flour (T65)
* 100 g (¾ cup/3½ oz) rye flour (T130)
* 325 g (1⅓ cups/11½ oz) water at 20°C (68°F)
* 9 g (1¾ tsp) Guérande sea salt
* 3 g (1 tsp) fresh yeast, crumbled

1. The previous day, combine 50 g (1¾ oz) of the flowers with the levain and rest overnight in the refrigerator to infuse the levain with a floral taste.

2. On the day, combine all the ingredients, except the remaining flowers, in a stand mixer fitted with a dough hook. Mix and knead for 4 minutes on low speed and then for 6 minutes on high speed. The dough should be smooth and come away from the sides of the bowl. Add the flowers and mix on low speed for 1 minute to incorporate without damaging them. Cover the mixer bowl with a cloth and leave the dough to rise for 2 hours at room temperature, folding after 1 hour.

3. On a floured work counter, divide the dough into two pieces of equal weight (about 560 g/1 lb 4 oz each) and loosely shape into balls. Cover with a cloth and rest for 15 minutes at room temperature.

4. Shape the dough pieces into boules (see page 30) without tightening at the seam. Place the boules on a floured cloth with the seam underneath. Cover with a cloth and prove (proof) for 2 hours at room temperature.

5. Place a baking pan on the lowest oven rack and preheat the oven to 250°C (480°F). Transfer the loaves to a baking sheet lined with baking (parchment) paper, with the seams facing upwards. Once the oven is hot, pour 50 ml (3½ tbsp/1¾ fl oz) water into the hot baking pan. Put the loaves and pan of water into the oven and bake for 20 minutes. Lower the temperature to 200°C (400°F) and bake for another 10 minutes.

6. Remove the loaves from the oven, then cool on a wire rack.

MIXED FRUIT AND NUT CROWN

MAKES 2 crowns

PREPARATION TIME 15 min

RESTING TIME 3 h 45 min

BAKING TIME 30 min

EQUIPMENT

* 2 couronne (ring) bannetons or 2 plain large bannetons

INGREDIENTS

* 280 g (10 oz) mixed fruit and nuts (or 30% of the weight of the dough): your choice of raisins, currants, dried figs, cranberries, apricots, prunes, hazelnuts, pecans, almonds, cashews, pine nuts or pistachios
* 500 g (scant 4 cups/1 lb 2 oz) plain (all-purpose) flour (T55)
* 325 g (1⅓ cups/11½ oz) water at 20°C (68°F)
* 100 g (scant ½ cup/3½ oz) Liquid Levain (see page 20)
* 5 g (1½ tsp) fresh yeast, crumbled
* 10 g (2 tsp) Guérande sea salt
* 30 g (2 tbsp/1 oz) softened butter

1. Preheat the oven to 240°C (465°F). Spread your choice of mixed nuts out on a baking sheet lined with baking (parchment) paper and toast for 10 minutes. Chop the larger ones roughly.

2. Chop the larger fruits (figs, prunes and apricots) into smallish dice. Mix all the dried fruit and nuts together in a mixing bowl.

3. Put the flour, water, levain, yeast and salt into a stand mixer fitted with a dough hook. Mix and knead for 5 minutes on low speed, then for 7 minutes on high speed. Mix in the butter and knead for another 3 minutes. Add the dried fruit and nuts and mix in briefly on low speed.

4. Gather the dough into a ball and cover with a damp cloth. Leave to rest for 1½ hours at room temperature. The dough will have increased in volume by the end of the resting time.

5. On a floured work counter, divide the dough into two equal pieces and shape them into balls. Cover with a damp cloth and rest for 15 minutes.

6. Working with one piece of dough at a time, use your fingers to make a large hole right through the middle. Working carefully, stretch and pull the dough as evenly as you can, to make the crown larger and larger until it reaches a diameter of around 30 cm (12 inches). Shape the second crown in the same way.

7. Place the crowns in floured banneton rings. Alternatively, sit a small bowl inside a large banneton and drape with a cloth to approximate the couronne. Cover with a damp cloth and prove (proof) for 2 hours at room temperature.

8. Place a baking pan on the lowest oven rack and preheat the oven to 230°C (450°F). Turn the crowns out onto 2 baking sheets lined with baking (parchment) paper. Score them however you like. Once the oven is hot, pour 50 ml (3½ tbsp/1¾ fl oz) water into the hot baking pan. Put the crowns and pan of water into the oven and bake for 20 minutes.

9. Remove the crowns from the oven, then cool on a wire rack.

MATCHA AND CANDIED ORANGE BREAD

MAKES 6 loaves

PREPARATION TIME 20 min

RESTING TIME 5 h 30 min

BAKING TIME 17 min

INGREDIENTS

* 10 g (3 tsp/¼ oz) matcha powder
* 500 g (scant 4 cups/1 lb 2 oz) white bread flour (T65)
* 500 g (3½ cups/1 lb 2 oz) cake (pastry) flour (T45/farine de gruau)
* 600 g (2½ cups/1 lb 5 oz) water at 16°C (60°F)
* 200 g (scant 1 cup/7 oz) Liquid Levain (see page 20)
* 30 g (2 tbsp/1 oz) caster (superfine) sugar
* 18 g (heaping 1 tbsp) Guérande sea salt
* 5 g (1½ tsp) fresh yeast, crumbled
* 60 g (6 tbsp/2¼ oz) olive oil + extra for finishing
* 200 g (1½ cups/7 oz) candied orange peel
* 1 egg, beaten, for glazing

1. Combine all the ingredients, except the olive oil, candied orange and egg, in a stand mixer fitted with a dough hook. Mix and knead for 5 minutes on low speed and then for 10 minutes on high speed. Add the olive oil, then incorporate the candied orange peel while mixing on low speed for 1 minute. Cover the mixer bowl with a cloth and leave the dough to rise for 3 hours at room temperature, folding after 1 hour.

2. On a floured work counter, divide the dough into six pieces of equal weight (about 350 g/12 oz each) and loosely shape into balls. Cover with a cloth and rest for 30 minutes at room temperature.

3. Shape the dough pieces into boules (see page 30). Transfer to a baking sheet lined with baking (parchment) paper, glaze by brushing with the beaten egg and score with a diamond cross-hatch (see page 37). Cover with a cloth and prove (proof) for 2 hours at room temperature.

4. Place a baking pan on the lowest oven rack and preheat the oven to 240°C (465°F). Once the oven is hot, pour 50 ml (3½ tbsp/1¾ fl oz) water into the hot baking pan. Put the loaves and pan of water into the oven and bake for 17 minutes.

5. Remove the loaves from the oven, brush them with a little olive oil and cool on a wire rack.

MATCHA AND CANDIED ORANGE BREAD

DATE AND CURRY BREAD

MAKES 7 loaves

PREPARATION TIME 20 min

RESTING TIME 4 h

BAKING TIME 20 min

INGREDIENTS

* 20 g (1 tbsp/¾ oz) curry powder
* 500 g (scant 4 cups/1 lb 2 oz) white bread flour (T65)
* 500 g (3½ cups/1 lb 2 oz) cake (pastry) flour (T45/farine de gruau)
* 650 g (2¾ cups/1 lb 7 oz) water at 16°C (60°F)
* 150 g (⅔ cup/5 oz) Liquid Levain (see page 20)
* 100 g (scant ⅓ cup/3½ oz) honey
* 5 g (1½ tsp) fresh yeast, crumbled
* 18 g (heaping 1 tbsp) Guérande sea salt
* 80 g (generous ⅓ cup/3 oz) coconut oil + extra for finishing
* 500 g (1 lb 2 oz) fresh Medjool dates, pitted and chopped

1. Combine all the ingredients, except the coconut oil and dates, in a stand mixer fitted with a dough hook. Mix and knead for 4 minutes on low speed and then for 8 minutes on high speed. Add the coconut oil and knead on low speed. Add the dates and mix for 2 minutes on low speed. Cover the mixer bowl with a cloth and leave the dough to rise for 2 hours at room temperature.

2. On a floured work counter, divide the dough into seven pieces of equal weight (about 350 g/12 oz each) and loosely shape into boules (see page 30). Transfer to a baking sheet lined with baking (parchment) paper, with the seams facing upwards. Cover with a cloth and prove (proof) for 2 hours at room temperature.

3. Place a baking pan on the lowest oven rack and preheat the oven to 220°C (425°F). Once the oven is hot, pour 50 ml (3½ tbsp/1¾ fl oz) water into the hot baking pan. Put the loaves and pan of water into the oven and bake for 20 minutes.

4. Remove the loaves from the oven, immediately brush the tops with a little coconut oil and cool on a wire rack.

BRIOCHES

PAIN AU LAIT

MAKES 7 buns

PREPARATION TIME 20 min

RESTING TIME 3 h 15 min

BAKING TIME 13–15 min

INGREDIENTS

* 500 g (scant 4 cups/1 lb 2 oz) white bread flour (T65)
* 230 g (scant 1 cup/8 oz) full-fat (whole) milk
* 20 g (2 tbsp) fresh yeast, crumbled
* 35 g (3 tbsp/1¼ oz) caster (superfine) sugar
* 10 g (2 tsp) Guérande sea salt
* 80 g (⅓ cup/3 oz) butter, softened and diced
* 1 egg, beaten, for glazing
* nibbed sugar, for decoration

1. In a stand mixer fitted with a dough hook, combine the flour with the milk, yeast, sugar and salt. Mix and knead for 4 minutes on low speed and then for 8 minutes on high speed. When the dough forms a ball and comes away from the sides of the bowl, gather it into a ball and add the butter. Knead until the dough is soft and smooth and comes away from the sides again. Gather the dough into a ball. Cover the mixer bowl with a slightly damp cloth and leave the dough to rise for 1 hour at room temperature. The dough should expand.

2. On a floured work counter, divide the dough into seven pieces of equal weight (about 130 g/4½ oz each). Cover with a cloth and rest for 15 minutes at room temperature.

3. Shape the dough pieces into bâtard loaves (see page 31) about 15 cm (6 inches) in length. Transfer to a baking sheet lined with baking (parchment) paper with the seam underneath. Brush the tops with beaten egg. Cover with a cloth and prove (proof) for 2 hours at room temperature.

4. Preheat the oven to 200°C (400°F). Brush the dough pieces with more egg. Score them with scissors dipped in egg: run the scissors over their length, snipping into the dough every centimetre (½ inch). Sprinkle with nibbed sugar and bake for 13–15 minutes.

5. Remove the buns from the oven, then cool on a wire rack.

WHITE CHOCOLATE BRIOCHE

MAKES 4 brioches

PREPARATION TIME 20 min

RESTING TIME 3 h

BAKING TIME 17 min

INGREDIENTS

* 500 g (scant 4 cups/1 lb 2 oz) white bread flour (T65)
* 225 g (scant 1 cup/8 oz) water at 16°C (60°F)
* 75 g (⅓ cup/2¾ oz) Liquid Levain (see page 20)
* 35 g (3 tbsp/1¼ oz) caster (superfine) sugar
* 25 g (1 oz) milk powder
* 10 g (2 tsp) Guérande sea salt
* 5 g (1½ tsp) fresh yeast, crumbled
* 75 g (⅓ cup/2¾ oz) butter, softened
* 150 g (scant 1 cup/5 oz) white chocolate chips
* 1 egg, beaten, for glazing

1 Combine all the ingredients, except the butter, chocolate chips and egg, in a stand mixer fitted with a dough hook. Mix and knead for 5 minutes on low speed and then for 8 minutes on high speed. When the dough is smooth and comes away from the sides of the bowl, incorporate the butter on low speed. Add the chocolate chips and mix for 2 minutes on the lowest speed. Cover the mixer bowl with a cloth and leave the dough to rise for 30 minutes at room temperature.

2 On a floured work counter, divide the dough into four pieces of equal weight (about 275 g/9¾ oz each). Loosely shape into balls. Cover with a cloth and rest for 30 minutes at room temperature.

3 Shape the dough pieces into bâtard loaves (see page 31). Transfer to a baking sheet lined with baking (parchment) paper. Brush the tops with beaten egg and immediately score them with the sausage cut (see page 34). Cover with a cloth and prove (proof) for 2 hours at room temperature.

4 Preheat the oven to 165°C (330°F). Bake for 17 minutes.

5 Remove the brioches from the oven, then cool on a wire rack.

CHOCOLATE AND BANANA BRIOCHE

MAKES 4 brioches

PREPARATION TIME 30 min

RESTING TIME 13 h 30 min

BAKING TIME 20–25 min

EQUIPMENT

* 4 loaf pans, 25 x 11 cm (10 x 4¼ inches)

FOR THE BRIOCHE

* 500 g (3½ cups/1 lb 2 oz) plain (all-purpose) flour (T55)
* 8 g (1½ tsp) Guérande sea salt
* 15 g (1½ tbsp) fresh yeast, crumbled
* 80 g (generous ⅓ cup/3 oz) caster (superfine) sugar
* 3 eggs + 1 beaten egg for glazing
* 125 g (½ cup/4¼ oz) full-fat (whole) milk
* 125 g (generous ½ cup/4½ oz) butter, softened and diced

FOR THE FILLING

* 125 g (generous ½ cup/4¼ oz) butter
* 175 g (6 oz) dark (semisweet) chocolate, broken into pieces
* 17 g (2½ tbsp/½ oz) unsweetened cocoa powder
* 80 g (generous ½ cup/3 oz) icing (confectioners') sugar
* 2 bananas, cut into pieces

FOR THE SYRUP

* 50 g (¼ cup/1¾ oz) caster (superfine) sugar
* 50 g (3½ tbsp/1¾ oz) water

1. The previous day, make the brioche dough. In a stand mixer fitted with a dough hook, put the flour and salt on one side, the yeast on the other, and then the sugar. Mix on low speed, adding the eggs, followed by the milk. Knead until the dough is smooth and pulls away from the sides of the bowl. Add the butter and knead on low speed until incorporated. The dough should be smooth and pull away from the sides of the bowl. Gather the dough into a ball, transfer to a bowl and cover with cling film (plastic wrap) in direct contact. Refrigerate overnight.

2. On the day, make the filling. Melt the butter and chocolate over a bain-marie (double boiler) or in the microwave. Mix in the cocoa and icing (confectioners') sugar until smooth. Let cool in the refrigerator (the filling will harden).

3. On a floured work counter, divide the dough into four pieces of equal weight (about 230 g/8 oz each). Using a rolling pin, roll them out into rectangles with the same length and three times the width of the loaf pan. Spread the filling and banana pieces over the top (a) and then tightly roll them up lengthways (b). Make cuts two-thirds of the way through every 2 cm (¾ inch) along their length (c). Spread the sections slightly apart, alternating their direction to resemble an ear of wheat (d). Place the dough pieces in the loaf pans, previously greased with butter and dusted with flour, then cover them with a damp cloth and prove (proof) for 1½ hours at room temperature. The dough should double in volume.

4. Preheat the oven to 180°C (350°F). Brush the brioches with beaten egg. Bake for 20–25 minutes. Halfway through baking or towards the end, cover the brioches with baking (parchment) paper if they colour too quickly.

5. In the meantime, make the syrup. Combine the sugar and water in a pan and bring to the boil. Remove from the heat.

6. Remove the brioches from the oven and brush them with syrup. Cool on a wire rack.

a

b

c

d

CHOCOLATE AND BANANA BRIOCHE

CHOCOLATE AND BANANA BRIOCHE

PLAITED (BRAIDED) BRIOCHE

MAKES 3 brioches

PREPARATION TIME 50 min

RESTING TIME 18 h

BAKING TIME 25 min

EQUIPMENT

* 3 loaf pans, 25 x 11 cm (10 x 4¼ inches)

FOR THE BRIOCHE

* 600 g (4¼ cups/1 lb 5 oz) cake (pastry) flour (T45/farine de gruau)
* 11 g (2 tsp) fine salt
* 22 g (generous 2 tbsp/¾ oz) fresh yeast, crumbled
* 85 g (scant ⅓ cup/3 oz) water at 20°C (68°F)
* 90 g (6 tbsp/3¼ oz) full-fat (whole) milk
* 5 eggs
* 90 g (scant ½ cup/3¼ oz) caster (superfine) sugar
* 10 g (2 tsp) dark rum
* 6 g (1 tsp) orange flower water
* 6 g (1 tsp) vanilla extract
* 140 g (scant ⅔ cup/5 oz) butter, softened

FOR THE FINISHING

* 1 egg, beaten, for glazing
* 1 tbsp full-fat (whole) milk
* pinch of fine salt

1. The previous day, mix 100 g (¾ cup/3½ oz) of the flour with 2 g (⅓ tsp) of the salt in a bowl, using a whisk. In a small bowl, dissolve 2 g (½ tsp) of the yeast in the water. Mix the dissolved yeast into the flour and salt mixture with a rubber spatula. Transfer the dough to a floured work counter and shape into a non-sticky ball. Put the dough into an airtight container with a lightly greased lid and refrigerate for at least 15 hours.

2. On the day, combine the milk with the eggs, sugar, rum, orange flower water and vanilla extract in a stand mixer fitted with a dough hook. Mix on low speed, then crumble in the remaining yeast and add the rest of the flour and knead on low speed until all ingredients are incorporated. Add the remaining salt while kneading. Incorporate the fermented dough from the previous day and mix on medium speed for 15 minutes until the dough comes away from the sides of the bowl. Gradually add the butter and knead for 15 minutes on high speed, until the dough again comes away from the sides. The dough should be smooth and glossy. Transfer to a lightly floured bowl, cover with cling film (plastic wrap) in direct contact and leave to rise for 30 minutes at room temperature. The dough should only rise slightly. Refrigerate for between 2 hours and overnight.

3. Preheat the oven to 30°C (86°F). On a floured work counter, divide the dough into nine pieces of equal weight (about 145 g/5¼ oz each). Roll them into uniform 25–30-cm (10–12-inch) strips (a) (b) (c) (d) (e). Place three strips vertically and seal them together at one end. Then plait (braid) them together (f) (g). Seal the other end and tuck both ends under (h). Repeat the operation to make two more brioches. Transfer the brioches into greased loaf pans and brush them with eggwash made by beating the egg, milk and salt together. Turn off the oven and put the brioches inside to prove (proof) for 1 to 1½ hours.

4. Remove the brioches and preheat the oven to 150°C (300°F). Glaze the brioches again with eggwash and bake for about 25 minutes, keeping an eye on them.

5. Remove the brioches from the oven, then cool on a wire rack.

a

b

c

d

PLAITED (BRAIDED) BRIOCHE

e

f

g

h

PLAITED (BRAIDED) BRIOCHE

EKMEK WITH RAISINS AND PECANS

MAKES 3 loaves

PREPARATION TIME 20 min

RESTING TIME 4 h 30 min

BAKING TIME 20 min

INGREDIENTS

* 500 g (scant 4 cups/1 lb 2 oz) white bread flour (T65)
* 275 g (1 cup plus 2 tbsp/9¾ oz) water at 16°C (60°F)
* 75 g (¼ cup/2¾ oz) honey
* 50 g (scant ¼ cup/1¾ oz) Liquid Levain (see page 20)
* 6 g (2 tsp) fresh yeast, crumbled
* 5 g (1 tbsp) ground cinnamon
* 9 g (1¾ tsp) Guérande sea salt
* 25 g (2½ tbsp/1 oz) olive oil + extra for finishing
* 90 g (¾ cup/3¼ oz) pecan nuts
* 90 g (⅔ cup/3¼ oz) raisins

1. Combine all the ingredients, except the olive oil, pecans and raisins in a stand mixer fitted with a dough hook. Mix and knead for 5 minutes on low speed and then for 8 minutes on high speed. The dough should be smooth and come away from the sides of the bowl. Incorporate the olive oil while kneading at a slow speed. Add the nuts and raisins, then mix for 2 minutes on low speed. Cover the mixer bowl with a cloth and leave the dough to rise for about 2 hours at room temperature.

2. On a lightly floured work counter, divide the dough into three pieces of equal weight (about 370 g/13 oz each). Loosely shape into balls. Cover with a cloth and rest for 30 minutes at room temperature.

3. Shape the dough pieces into boules (see page 30). Transfer to a baking sheet lined with baking (parchment) paper with the seam underneath. Cover with a cloth and prove (proof) for 2 hours at room temperature.

4. Place a baking pan on the lowest oven rack and preheat the oven to 220°C (425°F). Score the loaves with a diamond cross-hatch (see page 37). Once the oven is hot, pour 50 ml (3½ tbsp/1¾ fl oz) water into the hot baking pan. Put the loaves and pan of water into the oven and bake for 20 minutes.

5. Remove the loaves from the oven, immediately brush with olive oil and cool on a wire rack.

CHOCOLATE AND COCONUT EKMEK

MAKES 3 loaves

PREPARATION TIME 20 min

RESTING TIME 4 h 50 min

BAKING TIME 18 min

INGREDIENTS

* 425 g (scant 4 cups/15 oz) cake (pastry) flour (T45/farine de gruau)
* 50 g (½ cup/1¾ oz) coconut flour
* 325 g (1⅓ cups/11½ oz) water at 16°C (60°F)
* 50 g (3½ tbsp/1¾ oz) honey
* 75 g (⅓ cup/2¾ oz) Liquid Levain (see page 20)
* 9 g (1¾ tsp) Guérande sea salt
* 3 g (1 tsp) fresh yeast, crumbled
* 30 g (3 tbsp/1 oz) olive oil + extra for finishing
* 150 g (scant 1 cup/5 oz) dark (semisweet) chocolate chips
* 60 g (2¼ oz) coconut flakes
* 20 g (¾ oz) shredded coconut, for finishing

1 Combine all the ingredients, except the olive oil, chocolate chips and coconut, in a stand mixer fitted with a dough hook. Mix and knead for 4 minutes on low speed and then for 5 minutes on high speed. Incorporate the oil and mix for another 3 minutes. The dough should be smooth and pull away from the sides of the bowl. Finally, add the chocolate chips and coconut flakes, and mix for 2 minutes on low speed. Cover the mixer bowl with a cloth and leave the dough to rise for 2½ hours at room temperature, folding after 1¼ hours.

2 On a lightly floured work counter, divide the dough into three pieces of equal weight (about 380 g/13½ oz each). Loosely shape into balls. Cover with a cloth and rest for 20 minutes at room temperature.

3 Shape the dough pieces into boules (see page 30). Transfer to a baking sheet lined with baking (parchment) paper with the seam underneath. Cover with a cloth and prove (proof) for 2 hours at room temperature.

4 Place a baking pan on the lowest oven rack and preheat the oven to 220°C (425°F). Score the loaves with a diamond cross-hatch (see page 37). Once the oven is hot, pour 50 ml (3½ tbsp/1¾ fl oz) water into the hot baking pan. Put the ekmek and pan of water into the oven and bake for 18 minutes.

5 Remove from the oven, then immediately brush with olive oil. Sprinkle with shredded coconut and cool on a wire rack.

VIENNA BREAD WITH CHOCOLATE CHIPS

MAKES 9 loaves

PREPARATION TIME 25 min

RESTING TIME 2 h 45 min

BAKING TIME 20 min

EQUIPMENT

* Vienna trays (optional)

INGREDIENTS

* 500 g (scant 4 cups/1 lb 2 oz) white bread flour (T65)
* 260 g (generous 1 cup/9½ oz) water at 16°C (60°F)
* 75 g (⅓ cup/2¾ oz) butter, softened and diced
* 75 g (⅓ cup/2¾ oz) Liquid Levain (see page 20)
* 35 g (3 tbsp/1¼ oz) caster (superfine) sugar
* 25 g (1 oz) milk powder
* 9 g (1¾ tsp) Guérande sea salt
* 5 g (1½ tsp) fresh yeast, crumbled
* 150 g (scant 1 cup/5 oz) dark (semisweet) chocolate chips
* 1 egg, beaten, for glazing

1. Combine all the ingredients, except the chocolate chips and egg, in a stand mixer fitted with a dough hook. Mix and knead for 5 minutes on low speed and then for 10 minutes on high speed. The dough should pull away from the sides of the bowl and form a ball. Incorporate the chocolate chips and mix for 2 minutes on the lowest speed.

2. On a lightly floured work counter, divide the dough into nine pieces of equal weight (about 125 g/4½ oz each). Cover with a cloth and leave to rise for 30 minutes at room temperature.

3. Shape the dough pieces into small baguettes (see page 32). Deflate and tighten the dough. Transfer the loaves to the lightly greased Vienna or baking trays. Brush with beaten egg and rest in the refrigerator for 15 minutes.

4. Brush the loaves again with beaten egg and immediately score them with the sausage cut (see page 34). Cover with a cloth and prove (proof) for 2 hours at room temperature.

5. Preheat the oven to 170°C (340°F). Bake for 15 minutes. Remove the trays from the oven, turn the loaves over and bake for another 5 minutes to colour the underside.

6. Remove the loaves from the oven, then cool on a wire rack.

VIENNA BREAD WITH CHOCOLATE CHIPS

BABKA

MAKES 2 brioches

PREPARATION TIME 30 min

RESTING TIME 14 h 10 min–14 h 40 min

BAKING TIME 25–30 min

EQUIPMENT

* 2 loaf pans, 25 x 11 cm (10 x 4¼ inches)

FOR THE BRIOCHE

* 500 g (scant 4 cups/1 lb 2 oz) cake (pastry) flour (T45/farine de gruau)
* 200 g (scant 1 cup/7 oz) full-fat (whole) milk
* 3 eggs + 1 beaten egg for glazing
* 150 g (⅔ cup/5 oz) Liquid Levain (see page 20)
* 90 g (scant ½ cup/3¼ oz) caster (superfine) sugar
* 15 g (1½ tbsp) fresh yeast, crumbled
* 9 g (1¾ tsp) Guérande sea salt
* 160 g (scant ¾ cup/5 oz) butter, softened and diced

FOR THE FILLING

* 360 g (12½ oz) chocolate and hazelnut spread
* 80 g (scant ½ cup/3 oz) chocolate chips (or roasted hazelnuts)

FOR THE SYRUP

* 40 g (2½ tbsp/1½ oz) water
* 40 g (scant ¼ cup/1½ oz) caster (superfine) sugar

1. The previous day, combine all the brioche ingredients, except the egg for glazing and the butter, in a stand mixer fitted with a dough hook. Mix and knead on medium speed for about 10 minutes until the dough is smooth and pulls away from the sides of the bowl. Add the butter and knead on high speed until the dough pulls away from the sides again. Gather the dough into a ball and transfer to a greased or lightly floured bowl. Cover with a damp cloth and leave to rise for about 30 minutes at room temperature. Fold the dough, then refrigerate overnight.

2. On the day, with a rolling pin on a floured work counter, roll the dough out into a rectangle with the same length and three times the width of the loaf pan (a). Cover it with a layer of the spread and sprinkle with chocolate chips, reserving some for the top (b). Roll up the dough lengthways (c) and cut in half along the length to make two half-rolls. Set aside for 10 minutes in the freezer.

3. Cut the half-rolls in half again lengthways. Twist these two pieces together as if plaiting (braiding), with the cut side and exposed filling facing upwards (d). Place the plaited brioches into the greased loaf pans, lined with baking (parchment) paper, and sprinkle with the remaining chocolate chips. Cover with a cloth and prove (proof) for 1½ to 2 hours at room temperature.

4. Preheat the oven to 160°C (325°F). Brush the brioches with beaten egg. Bake for 25–30 minutes.

5. In the meantime, make the syrup. Combine the water and sugar in a pan and bring to the boil.

6. Remove the brioches from the oven, let cool for 5 minutes and turn them out. Brush the babkas with syrup.

a

b

c

d

COCONUT BRIOCHE

MAKES 4 brioches

PREPARATION TIME 20 min

RESTING TIME 4 h 30 min– 4 h 45 min

BAKING TIME 25 min

INGREDIENTS

* 80 g (½ cup/3 oz) coconut sugar
* 500 g (3½ cups/1 lb 2 oz) plain (all-purpose) flour (T55)
* 220 g (1 cup/7¾ oz) crème fraîche
* 2 eggs + 1 beaten egg for glazing
* 15 g (1½ tbsp) fresh yeast, crumbled
* 9 g (1¾ tsp) Guérande sea salt
* 50 g (¼ cup/1¾ oz) coconut oil
* 100 g (scant ½ cup/3½ oz) butter, softened and diced

1. Combine all the ingredients, except the coconut oil, beaten egg for glazing and butter, in a stand mixer fitted with a dough hook. Mix on low speed for 5 minutes until the dough is smooth and pulls away from the sides of the bowl. Incorporate the coconut oil and butter on low speed. The dough should pull away from the sides while remaining slightly sticky. Cover the mixer bowl with a cloth and leave the dough to rise for 2 hours at room temperature.

2. On a floured work counter, divide the dough into four pieces of equal weight (about 270 g/9½ oz each). Loosely shape the dough pieces into balls and place on a tray. Refrigerate for 30–45 minutes.

3. Shape the dough pieces into boules (see page 30), tightening well. Transfer to a baking sheet lined with baking (parchment) paper. Cover with a cloth and prove (proof) for 2 hours at room temperature.

4. Preheat the oven to 150°C (300°F). Brush the brioches with beaten egg and bake for 25 minutes.

5. Remove the brioches from the oven, then cool on a wire rack.

COCONUT BRIOCHE

JAPANESE MILK BREAD WITH WHITE CHOCOLATE

MAKES 2 loaves

PREPARATION TIME 25 min

RESTING TIME 4 h 30 min

BAKING TIME 30–40 min

EQUIPMENT
* 2 loaf pans, 25 x 11 cm (10 x 4¼ inches)

INGREDIENTS
* 500 g (3½ cups/1 lb 2 oz) cake (pastry) flour (T45/farine de gruau)
* 300 g (1¼ cups/10½ oz) water at 16°C (60°F)
* 75 g (⅓ cup/2¾ oz) Liquid Levain (see page 20)
* 9 g (1¾ tsp) Guérande sea salt
* 60 g (generous ¼ cup/2¼ oz) caster (superfine) sugar
* 60 g (2¼ oz) milk powder
* 6 g (2 tsp) fresh yeast, crumbled
* 10 g (2 tsp/¼ oz) crème fraîche
* 75 g (⅓ cup/2¾ oz) butter, softened
* 22 g (scant ¼ cup/¾ oz) unsweetened cocoa powder
* 80 g (scant ½ cup/3 oz) white chocolate chips
* 1 egg, beaten, for glazing
* icing (confectioners') sugar, for dusting

1 In a stand mixer fitted with a dough hook, combine the flour with the water, levain, salt, caster (superfine) sugar, milk powder and yeast. Mix and knead for 4 minutes on low speed to a smooth dough, then for 13 minutes on high speed. The dough should be smooth and form a ball that pulls away from the sides of the bowl. Add the crème fraîche and butter while mixing on low speed until fully incorporated. The dough should pull away from the sides while remaining slightly sticky. Add the cocoa powder and knead for 2 minutes on medium speed. Add the white chocolate chips and knead for 1 minute on low speed to incorporate. Cover the mixer bowl with a cloth and leave the dough to rise for 30 minutes at room temperature.

2 On a floured work counter, divide the dough into four pieces of equal weight (about 300 g/10½ oz each). Loosely shape the dough pieces into balls and place on a tray. Refrigerate for 1 hour.

3 Shape the dough pieces into boules, tightening well (see page 30). Fill each loaf pan with 2 boules. Cover with a cloth and prove (proof) for 2 hours at room temperature.

4 Preheat the oven to 160°C (325°F). Brush the loaves with beaten egg and bake for 30–40 minutes.

5 Remove the loaves from the oven, then cool on a wire rack. Dust with icing (confectioners') sugar.

JAPANESE MILK BREAD WITH PISTACHIOS AND CHERRIES

MAKES 2 loaves

PREPARATION TIME 25 min

RESTING TIME 4 h

BAKING TIME 30–40 min

EQUIPMENT

* 2 loaf pans, 25 x 11 cm (10 x 4¼ inches)

INGREDIENTS

* 500 g (3½ cups/1 lb 2 oz) cake (pastry) flour (T45/farine de gruau)
* 300 g (1¼ cups/10½ oz) water at 16°C (60°F)
* 75 g (⅓ cup/2¾ oz) Liquid Levain (see page 20)
* 9 g (1¾ tsp) Guérande sea salt
* 60 g (4 tbsp/2¼ oz) caster (superfine) sugar
* 60 g (2¼ oz) milk powder
* 6 g (2 tsp) fresh yeast, crumbled
* 50 g (3½ tbsp/1¾ oz) crème fraîche
* 75 g (⅓ cup/2¾ oz) butter, softened
* 55 g (2 oz) pistachio paste
* 100 g (¾ cup/3½ oz) dried cherries, pitted and chopped
* 50 g (⅓ cup/1¾ oz) pistachios, chopped
* 1 egg, beaten, for glazing

1. In a stand mixer fitted with a dough hook, combine the flour with the water, levain, salt, sugar, milk powder and yeast. Mix and knead for 4 minutes on low speed to a smooth dough, then for 13 minutes on high speed. The dough should be smooth and form a ball that pulls away from the sides of the bowl. Add the crème fraîche and butter while mixing on low speed until fully incorporated. The dough should pull away from the sides while remaining slightly sticky. Add the pistachio paste and knead for 2 minutes on medium speed. Add the cherries and knead for 1 minute on low speed. Cover the mixer bowl with a cloth and leave the dough to rise for 30 minutes at room temperature.

2. On a floured work counter, divide the dough into four pieces of equal weight (about 300 g/10½ oz each). Loosely shape the dough pieces into balls and place on a tray. Refrigerate for 1 hour.

3. Shape the dough pieces into boules, tightening well (see page 30). Fill each loaf pan with 2 boules. Cover with a cloth and prove (proof) for 2½ hours at room temperature.

4. Preheat the oven to 160°C (325°F). Brush the loaves with beaten egg and sprinkle with the chopped pistachios. Bake for 30–40 minutes.

5. Remove the loaves from the oven, then cool on a wire rack.

INDEXES

INDEX BY RECIPE

BABKA	202
BAGEL	134
BAGUETTE	48
BAO	126
BOULE	44
BRAN LOAF	102
BUCKWHEAT AND SEED BREAD	74
BURGER BUNS	124
CASSEROLE BREAD	62
CHALLAH	146
CHEESE BREAD	156
CHESTNUT BREAD	92
CHOCOLATE AND BANANA BRIOCHE	186
CHOCOLATE AND COCONUT EKMEK	197
CIABATTA WITH SUN-DRIED TOMATOES AND BASIL	144
COCONUT BRIOCHE	206
CORN AND SUNFLOWER SEED BREAD	94
DANISH BREAD	76
DATE AND CURRY BREAD	178
EINKORN BREAD	68
EKMEK WITH RAISINS AND PECANS	196
FIG, HAZELNUT AND FENNEL BREAD	168
FLOWER BREAD	172
FOUGASSE WITH GOAT CHEESE	148
GRAPE SEED BREAD	96
HEMP BREAD	114
HERITAGE WHEAT BREAD	82
JAPANESE MILK BREAD WITH PISTACHIOS AND CHERRIES	209
JAPANESE MILK BREAD WITH WHITE CHOCOLATE	208
KAMUT® BREAD	106
LENTIL AND CHICKPEA FLOUR BREAD	112
LUPIN AND ALMOND BREAD	104
MATCHA AND CANDIED ORANGE BREAD	176
MIXED FRUIT AND NUT CROWN	174
NAAN	130
NO-KNEAD BREAD	56
NORWEGIAN BREAD	78
OLIVE BREAD	162
PAIN AU LAIT	182
PITTA	132
PIZZA	122
PLAITED (BRAIDED) BRIOCHE	190
QUINOA FLOUR BREAD	116
RICE FLOUR AND BUCKWHEAT BREAD	90
ROSEMARY FOCACCIA	140
RYE LOAF	64
SEMOLINA BREAD	98
SESAME BREAD	80
SPELT AND SEED BREAD	72
SPELT BREAD	108
SWEET POTATO FLOUR BREAD	118
TABATIERE	50
THREE-GRAIN LOAF	66
TORTILLA	138
THE TWIST	150
VIENNA BREAD WITH CHOCOLATE CHIPS	200
WALNUT AND BUTTER BREAD	158
WALNUT, HAZELNUT AND TURMERIC BREAD	166
WHITE CHOCOLATE BRIOCHE	184
WHOLEMEAL BREAD	54
WREATH	58
ZIGZAG BREAD	86

INDEX

Note: Page references in *italics* indicate photographs.

A

almond and lupin bread	104, *105*
ash content	12

B

babka	202–3, *205*
bagel	134–35, *136–37*
BAGUETTE	
recipe for	48, *49*
shaping dough for	32
baker's cloths	24
baker's lame	24
baking paper	24
baking the bread	26
banana and chocolate brioche	186–88, *189*
bannetons	24
bao	126–27, *128–29*
barley flour	16
basil and sun-dried tomatoes, ciabatta with	144, *145*
bâtard, shaping	31
bench rest	26
BOULE	
pre-shaping	29
recipe for	44–45, *46–47*
shaping	30
bran loaf	102, *103*
BREAD MAKING	
bread-maker's lexicon	38–39
troubleshooting	40
BREAD-MAKING STAGES	
baking	26
bench rest	26
dividing and shaping	26
final shaping	26
first rise	26
folding	28
mixing and kneading	26
pre-shaping	26, 29
proving (proofing)	26
removing and cooling	26
scoring (cutting)	26, 34–37
shaping	30–33
BRIOCHE	
babka	202–3, *205*
chocolate and banana brioche	186–88, *189*
chocolate and coconut ekmek	197, *198–99*
coconut brioche	206, *207*
ekmek with raisins and pecans	196, *198–99*
Japanese milk bread with pistachios and cherries	209, *210*
Japanese milk bread with white chocolate	208, *210*
pain au lait	182, *183*
plaited (braided) brioche	190–93, *194–95*
Vienna bread with chocolate chips	200, *201*
white chocolate brioche	184, *185*
BUCKWHEAT FLOUR	
about	16
buckwheat and seed bread	74, *75*
rice flour and buckwheat bread	90, *91*
three-grain loaf	66, *67*
BUNS	
bao	126–27, *128–29*
burger buns	124, *125*
BUTTER	
babka	202–3, *205*
chocolate and banana brioche	186–88, *189*
coconut brioche	206, *207*
Japanese milk bread with pistachios and cherries	209, *210*
Japanese milk bread with white chocolate	208, *210*
pain au lait	182, *183*
plaited (braided) brioche	190–93, *194–95*
Vienna bread with chocolate chips	200, *201*
walnut and butter bread	158–59, *161*
white chocolate brioche	184, *185*

C

cake/pastry flour	12
casserole bread	62, *63*
challah	146, *147*
CHEESE	
cheese bread	156, *157*
cheese naan	130
fougasse with goat cheese	148, *149*
pizza	122, *123*
cherries and pistachios, Japanese milk bread with	209, *210*
chestnut bread	92, *93*

CHESTNUT FLOUR	
about	16
chestnut bread	92, *93*
CHICKPEA (GRAM) FLOUR	
about	16
lentil and chickpea flour bread	112, *113*
CHOCOLATE	
babka	202–3, *205*
chocolate and banana brioche	186–88, *189*
chocolate and coconut ekmek	197, *198–99*
Japanese milk bread with white chocolate	208, *210*
Vienna bread with chocolate chips	200, *201*
white chocolate brioche	184, *185*
ciabatta with sun-dried tomatoes and basil	144, *145*
cloths and dish towels	24
COCONUT	
chocolate and coconut ekmek	197, *198–99*
coconut brioche	206, *207*
common wheat	12
corn and sunflower seed bread	94, *95*
CRÈME FRAÎCHE	
coconut brioche	206, *207*
fougasse with goat cheese	148, *149*
curry and date bread	178, *179*

D

Danish bread	76, *77*
dark wholemeal (whole wheat) flour	12
date and curry bread	178, *179*
digital scales	24
dish towels	24
dividing and shaping the dough	26
dough scraper	24
durum wheat	12

E

EINKORN FLOUR	
about	16
einkorn bread	68, *69*
Norwegian bread	78, *79*
quinoa flour bread	116, *117*
three-grain loaf	66, *67*
EKMEK	
chocolate and coconut ekmek	197, *198–99*
ekmek with raisins and pecans	196, *198–99*
equipment	24

F

fennel, fig, and hazelnut bread	168, *169–71*
fig, hazelnut and fennel bread	168, *169–71*
final shaping of the dough	26
first rise for the dough	26
FLOURS. *See also specific types*	
with gluten	16
gluten-free	16
types of	12–16
flower bread	172, *173*
focaccia, rosemary	140–41, *142–43*
folding the dough	28
fougasse with goat cheese	148, *149*
FRUIT. *See also specific fruits*	
mixed fruit and nut crown	174, *175*

G

gluten content	12
gluten-free flours	16

GRAPE SEED FLOUR	
about	16
grape seed bread	96, *97*
grignette	24

H

HAM	
pizza	122, *123*
HAZELNUTS	
Danish bread	76, *77*
fig, hazelnut and fennel bread	168, *169–71*
walnut, hazelnut and turmeric bread	166, *167*
HEMP SEEDS	
hemp bread	114, *115*
heritage wheat bread	82–83, *84–85*

I

ingredients	18
See also FLOURS	

J

Japanese milk bread with pistachios and cherries	209, *210*
Japanese milk bread with white chocolate	208, *210*

K

KAMUT® FLOUR
  about   12
  Kamut® bread   106, *107*

L

LENTIL FLOUR
  about   16
  lentil and chickpea flour bread, 112   *113*
LEVAIN
  dehydrated   18
  liquid, about   18
  liquid, preparing   20
  stiff, about   18
  stiff, preparing   23
light wholemeal (whole wheat) flour   12
LINSEED
  spelt and seed bread   72, *73*
loaves, pre-shaping   29
LUPIN FLOUR
  about   16
lupin and almond bread   104, *105*

M

MAIZE FLOUR
  about   16
corn and sunflower seed bread   94, *95*
matcha and candied orange bread   176, *177*
millet flour   16
mixed fruit and nut crown   174, *175*
mixing and kneading the dough   26
mixing bowls   24

N

NAAN
  cheese naan   130
  naan   130, *131*
  seeded naan   130
no-knead bread   56, *57*
Norwegian bread   78, *79*
NUTS. See also specific nuts
  adding to breads   16
  mixed fruit and nut crown   174, *175*

O

oat flour   16
olive bread   162–63, *164–65*
orange, candied, and matcha bread   176, *177*
ORANGE FLOWER WATER
  plaited (braided)
  brioche   190–93, *194–95*

P

pain au lait   182, *183*
pans and moulds   24
PAVÉ LOAVES
  pre-shaping   29
  shaping   33
pecans and raisins, ekmek with   196, *198–99*
pistachios and cherries,
Japanese milk bread with   209, *210*
pitta   132, *133*
pizza   122, *123*
plain flour   12
plaited (braided)
brioche   190–93, *194–95*

POPCORN
  corn and sunflower
  seed bread   94, *95*
POPPY SEEDS
  bagel   134–35, *136–37*
  challah   146, *147*
  spelt and seed bread   72, *73*
pre-shaping the dough   26, 29
proving the dough   26
PUMPKIN SEEDS
  Danish bread   76, *77*
  spelt and seed bread   72, *73*
  sweet potato flour bread   118, *119*

Q

QUINOA FLOUR
  about   16
  quinoa flour bread   116, *117*

R

RAISINS
  ekmek with raisins
  and pecans   196, *198–99*
  grape seed bread   96, *97*
RICE FLOUR
  about   16
  hemp bread   114, *115*
  rice flour and buckwheat
  bread   90, *91*
rosemary focaccia   140–41, *142–43*
RUM
  plaited (braided)
  brioche   190–93, *194–95*
RYE FLOUR
  about   16
  bran loaf   102, *103*
  Danish bread   76, *77*
  flower bread   172, *173*
  rye loaf   64, *65*
  three-grain loaf   66, *67*
  wreath   58–59, *60–61*
  zigzag bread   86, *87*

S

salt	18
scales, digital	24
scoring (cutting) the dough	26, 34–37

SEEDS. *See also specific seeds*
- adding to breads — 16
- buckwheat and seed bread — 74, *75*
- Norwegian bread — 78, *79*
- seeded naan — 130
- spelt and seed bread — 72, *73*

SEMOLINA
- about — 12
- semolina bread — 98, *99*

SESAME SEEDS
- bagel — 134–35, *136–37*
- burger buns — 124, *125*
- challah — 146, *147*
- Danish bread — 76, *77*
- sesame bread — 80, *81*
- spelt and seed bread — 72, *73*

SHAPING THE DOUGH
- baguette — 32
- bâtard — 31
- boules — 30
- pavé — 33
- pre-shaping — 26, 29

SPELT FLOUR
- about — 16
- spelt and seed bread — 72, *73*
- spelt bread — 108–10, *111*

stand mixer — 24

SUNFLOWER SEEDS
- corn and sunflower seed bread — 94, *95*
- Danish bread — 76, *77*
- spelt and seed bread — 72, *73*

SWEET POTATO FLOUR
- about — 16
- sweet potato flour bread — 118, *119*

T

tabatiere	50, *52–53*
three-grain loaf	66, *67*
tomatoes, sun-dried, and basil,	
ciabatta with	144, *145*
tortilla	138, *139*
turmeric, walnut and hazelnut bread	166, *167*
the twist	150–51, *153*

U

utensils, small — 24

V

Vienna bread with chocolate chips — 200, *201*

W

WALNUTS
- Danish bread — 76, *77*
- walnut, hazelnut and turmeric bread — 166, *167*
- walnut and butter bread — 158–59, *161*

water — 18

WHEAT BRAN. *See* BRAN LOAF

WHEAT FLOUR. SEE ALSO SPECIFIC TYPES
- gluten content — 12
- T number — 12
- types of — 12

white bread flour — 12

WHITE CHOCOLATE
- Japanese milk bread with white chocolate — 208, *210*
- white chocolate brioche — 184, *185*

WHOLEMEAL (WHOLE WHEAT) FLOUR
- about — 12
- Danish bread — 76, *77*
- grape seed bread — 96, *97*
- lupin and almond bread — 104, *105*
- Norwegian bread — 78, *79*
- wholemeal (whole wheat) bread — 54, *55*
- wreath — 58–59, *60–61*

Y

yeast, fresh — 18, 20

Z

zigzag bread — 86, *87*

Phaidon Press Limited
2 Cooperage Yard
London E15 2QR

Phaidon Press Inc.
65 Bleecker Street
New York, NY 10012

phaidon.com

First published 2022
© 2022 Phaidon Press Limited

ISBN 978 1 83866 574 6

The Bread Book originates from *Le Grand Livre du Pain* by Éric Kayser © Larousse 2021, with the exception of pages 44–53, 86–87, 102–103, 108–111, 148–151, 153, 158–161, 174–175, which originate from *Le Larousse du Pain* by Éric Kayser © Larousse 2013.

A CIP catalogue record for this book is available from the British Library and the Library of Congress.

All rights reserved. No part of this publication may be reproduced, stored in a retrieval system or transmitted, in any form or by any means, electronic, mechanical, photocopying, recording or otherwise, without the written permission of Phaidon Press Limited.

COMMISSIONING EDITORS
Emilia Terragni and Emily Takoudes

PROJECT EDITOR
Michelle Meade

PRODUCTION CONTROLLER
Lily Rodgers

DESIGN
Julia Hasting

LAYOUTS
Cantina

PHOTOGRAPHY
Massimo Pessina

COVER PHOTOGRAPHY
Hélène Gallois Montbrun

ORIGINAL COVER PHOTOGRAPHY
Massimo Pessina

Printed in China

ACKNOWLEDGMENTS

Éric Kayser would like to thank Élodie De Montbron, Richard Boussuge, Jawad Abouassam, Gérard Boulanger, Ali Binkdan, Christophe Rouault and Claudia Sobrecases for their invaluable assistance in the creation of this work.

Phaidon would like to thank James Brown, Hélène Gallois Montbrun, Julia Hasting, João Mota, Elizabeth Parson, Sally Somers, Ellie Smith, Kathy Steer and Ana Teodoro.

AUTHOR BIO

Hailed as one of France's best bakers, Éric Kayser comes from a long line of French bakers and is the founder of the award-winning international bakery chain Maison Kayser. His cookbook *The Larousse Book of Bread* has been translated into eight languages, sold 200,000 copies worldwide and inspired a new generation of breadmakers with classic bread and pastry recipes.

RECIPE NOTES

Butter is unsalted, unless specified otherwise.

Herbs are fresh, unless specified otherwise.

Eggs are assumed to be large (US extra large) and preferably organic and free-range.